Sales
HR
Strategy

Managing Sales HR for Enhanced Business Performance

Ritesh Agarwal

MBA (HR)- XLRI Jamshedpur, India
SHRM-SCP, ATD-CPLP

Title: Sales HR Strategy
Author: Ritesh Agarwal

ISBN: 979-8-64-015966-0

Dedication

This book is dedicated to every reader who wants to build a salesforce, not a mere salesman.

Contents

Blank Page

Acknowledgements

This book is an experience and I am immensely thankful to all the leaders and friends in Sales who have contributed to my experiences, which helped me understand the importance of Sales HR Strategy.

A special thanks is always reserved for all my family members and friends who have encouraged me and have also been my toughest critics. Without their constant support, I would not have been able to give words to my varied experiences.

A special mention of my friend- Prof. Gaurav Marathe who graciously agreed to review the book and share his perspective and Rahul Khullar who has been a pillar of strength and constant help.

Lastly, thanks to my wife- Kirti Parasrampuria Agarwal (MBA-Finance, B.Ed., B.A. (English Hons.)), my sister Shruti Sureka (C.A., C.S., B.Com.) & my friend Garima Bawa Alag (MBA(HR)- XLRI Jamshedpur, SPHR, CPLP, SHRM-SCP, B.A.(Hons.)-Psychology) for proof-reading my entire book and adding their flavor to make it interesting.

Foreword

To predict a certain future, you don't need to know astrological stars or analytical tools; the star qualities demonstrated by an individual in the forming days are sufficient! Knowing commitment and competence of Ritesh Agarwal for more than decade starting as an MBA classmate in XLRI in 2008, it is no surprise that the book written by Ritesh reflects his quest for excellence and perfection in whichever task he takes on his shoulders. The book brings out insightful pearls of wisdom synthesized by mapping rigorous decade long experience and exposure of sales HR and continuous passionate learning of HR knowledge simultaneously in detailed and structured manner.

I don't hesitate to say that Ritesh has just produced a Bible for any future Sales HR managers helping them to accelerate their learning curve significantly. The book is void of even a single line which has no linkage to the work done by Sales HR and is direct reflection of focused and meticulous attitude of author in his personal and professional life. In very systematic manner providing every, small and large valuable insights that is critical to manage several employee touch points, Ritesh takes us through entire HR life cycle of sales employees starting from workforce planning, recruitment, selection, onboarding, capability building, performance management, rewards, engagement, motivation, career planning, and exit.

While the book integrates HR theories coherently in the context of Sales HR, some insights given in the book such as providing advance salaries on first day of joining so that an employee can manage cash flows at any new location or a checklist of onboarding content are only possible with decade long experience that Ritesh holds in the field and no traditional textbook is capable of giving those pieces.

Each chapter ends with a carefully crafted summary and business-related scenario case studies making it a wholesome learning experience for the readers and giving them time to critically reflect and connect back *what they have learnt till that point. It is assumed that tacit knowledge is generally hard to be written down and can't be transferred easily highlighting important value of actually having that work experience directly. However, reading Ritesh's reflection on his experience in HR seems to be breaking that assumption.*

This book is a significant resource for anyone managing or having an intent to manage the dynamic domain of Sales HR. This small 100+ pages book represents the dense and in-depth tacit knowledge written with a razor focused intent and arranged in a systematic structure for easy consumption, giving the readers delight and satisfaction of reading!

Prof. Gaurav Manohar Marathe

Professor (Organization Behavior) at Indian Institute of Management, Ranchi
Fellow of Management, XLRI (Organizational Behavior)

Preface

Sales function is the most important revenue generating function for any organization. The importance of this function is higher in companies that are in the space of consumer goods, pharmaceutical, banking, financial services, insurance services, retail, electronic products, software/IT services or have retail space requiring a large sales team. While the size of the sales team may vary based on the business models, types of products or services and many other factors, what remains constant is the importance of effectively managing and supporting the sales team through a robust Human Resources (HR) strategy.

This book focuses on the practical aspects of building a 'Human Resources Plan' for the sales team, especially in the consumer products sector. The concepts mentioned in this book are the result of years of experience of working with various sales teams across multiple geographies and learnings from handling complex people issues. The concepts can be easily leveraged for sales teams in any other sector as the core needs of the sales people working in any organization largely remain the same.

This book highlights the key people decisions that needs to be made to ensure a smooth employee life cycle in the sales function to drive business performance. The book is written in an easy to comprehend manner and divided into small chapters which address the various HR processes in Sales. Starting with discussion on workforce planning and followed by elaboration on the important HR functions (like recruitment & selection, on-boarding, capability building, talent & performance management, providing careers, employee engagement, compensation & incentives, attrition or turnover management, grievance management & ethics, safety & legal aspects, and finally, retirement/termination) this book highlights the key aspects in making a sound HR Strategy in each of these critical HR processes.

The book has the last two chapters dedicated on two most important needs of any business in this modern age- managing teams across cultures and countries as organizations continue to expand beyond their countries of origin; and preparing for uncertain business situations. Each chapter is followed by an open-case study to stimulated thinking, discussion and learning and a summary to highlight the key points of the chapter.

This book can be read by any professional but will be most beneficial to:

1. Students of Human Resources Management in Management Institutes who can get a flair of the corporate world.
2. New HR professionals entering corporate jobs (like HR Business Partner for Sales).
3. Practicing HR professionals & CHROs.
4. Entrepreneurs who are setting up their sales teams & systems from scratch.
5. Sales leaders deciding on key people areas.

The book assumes that the reader is aware of the basic concepts of human resources management and thus focusses only on practical aspects for every HR process. I have presented generic business situations for educational purposes and these views are my own, not specific to any company, organization or person I am associated with. Also, although I would have preferred to use a gender-neutral language, however, the pronouns used are in male format for my ease of writing.

I look forward to your comments, feedback and insights on this book on Amazon.com or via email to inspire@riteshagarwal.org.

Happy Reading!

Ritesh Agarwal

Chapter 1: Elements of Sales HR Strategy

> *"I believe the real difference between success and failure in a corporation can be very often traced to the question of how well the organization brings out the great energies and talents of its people."*
> — *Thomas J. Watson, Jr.*

Sales function in any medium and large-scale organizations consists of sizeable number of sales employees spread across multiple geographies, looking after numerous product lines and servicing multiple clients. Even in small-scale organizations, the sales team is responsible to drive the sales of products and generate revenues for the company. In a start-up, the importance of an effective sales team is even more and is a make or break factor for the sustenance of the company.

The sales team is the face of any company and the importance given to this function reflects the culture and defines the success of that company. Managing HR aspects of such an important and diverse team is a complex task. Adding to this complexity is the fact that if anything goes wrong, it will immediately impact business revenues, profits, market share and eventually credibility of the company in the market and the stock exchange.

In order to create a robust Sales HR Strategy, firstly, the business goals, vision, mission and the organization's & market's culture must be understood thoroughly. Detailed analysis of business targets, nature of product, customer profiles, competitors, vendors/partners, compliances, taxes, internal policies, overall business environment, etc. should be done. As a Sales Human Resource Business Partner (or Sales HRBP), it is then important to use these inputs to create a HR Strategy and define the structure and workflow of the important HR processes. Any Sales HR Strategy is not a stand-alone work but needs to evolve from these important aspects of business. This helps to create a well-rounded Sales HR Strategy that can be implemented to have a fully functioning sales team.

The image (I1.1) highlights the key elements of Sales HR Strategy outlined above. It summarizes the key inputs, outputs and the various enablers for the plan.

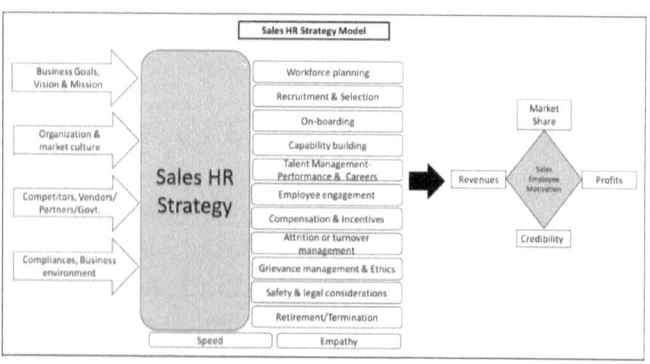

Image I1.1

An important enabler of the Sales HR Strategy is the speed with which people decisions need to be taken for sales teams to address business issues. The margin of error for Sales HRBP is very low and even business has a lot of dependence on their actions and inactions. In managing these strategic aspects, one must not forget to be empathetic and approach any business problem from a human angle.

In any sales environment, HR decisions generally revolve around the following critical roles-

1. Sales Representatives or Salesmen.
2. Sales Supervisors or first line Sales Managers.
3. Sales Managers or Manager of managers.
4. Sales Director or Head of Sales.

These roles can vary in their responsibilities based on the customer types that they service (e.g. retailers in general trade vs. big customers in organized trade or servicing direct consumers) & the nature of products or services they are selling. The number of employees doing the above roles generally reduces as we move up the hierarchy from salesman to sales director and hence HR strategy and process complexity need to be tailored basis the headcount number.

Ensuing chapters can help you plan the various HR processes for the sales team in an effective and easy to implement manner. **A robust HR Strategy is a critical cornerstone to a robust business performance.**

Blank Page

Chapter 2: Workforce Planning

> *"One machine can do the work of fifty ordinary men. No machine can do the work of one extraordinary man."*
> *– Elbert Hubbard*

The importance of Sales HR Strategy is best realized when the team size is big. Often, hiring any candidate for a role without due diligence and loosely defined responsibilities is a recipe for disaster. Workforce planning is the first and the most important element of the entire HR Plan. Hence, enough time and thinking should go into this crucial step.

It has been observed that in many organizations, workforce planning is a decision unilaterally taken by business heads and is based on their ambition of growth than on objective principles. Human resource professionals are often not involved in the workforce planning and even if they are, the expectation is more from an execution perspective. This creates a pressure on the HRBPs to first hire at a fast pace, set up HR processes with little alignment to HR Strategy and then, when things do not result into improved sales, they are forced to lay-off to save costs. The vicious circle of hiring and firing continues. This impacts the credibility of the company, reduces its employee proposition in the market and spoils the credibility of the HR leader. Remember, all organization issues begin with hiring more people than required.

Voice of HR on the table is important

The best way to avoid situations like above is to make it clear to the business stakeholders that any people related decisions cannot be taken without including the Sales HRBP right from the planning process. This is a tough thing to do if it has not happened in the past or the company's existing culture doesn't include HR in key decision making.

Smart HRBPs should identify opportunities in such situations and build credibility by highlighting the facts, figures and key data from the ground which could facilitate in making such decisions. Few important metrics that can help are:

1. Volume/Value/Revenue plans per sales employee in the current context.
2. Actual Volume/Value/Revenue delivered per sales employee in the recent past.
3. The reason of gaps if any in the above numbers.
4. Ideal Span for each Supervisor/Manager to manage the team in the best possible manner.
5. Any past evidence of increase in sales attributed to the increase in headcount.
6. If possible, get the competitor data on the above and show the difference.
7. Ideal number of customers/clients/outlets that can be serviced by each employee basis time motion studies.

More people don't always result into better performance

An important aspect is to Not assume that hiring more employees will translate into proportionate increase in sales. People should not be considered pseudo-machines which once installed will generate consistent results or run with a pre-defined speed. Often it takes weeks, in cases months, to bring people to speed and deliver the desired performance levels.

While everybody knows these factors well, but the ambition to drive things faster and deliver quick results often make the best of business leaders and sometimes HR leaders skip logical 'Workforce Planning' and that often results into hiring too many people than required. Sales HRBPs should bear in mind that hiring more employees is always the easier part but managing the stress on people operations due to increased number of employees is far difficult. Further, often things don't go well culminating into downsizing.

The best way to address this situation is to always agree with the management on the metrics or key performance indicators ("KPI's") that need to be used if a certain hiring decision is made. Some of the points that can be considered are:

1. What will be the target change in sales performance with increase in headcount? (e.g. Will adding 5 more headcounts result into 10% sales increase or 15% sales increase?)
2. What will be the onboarding/training hours of the employee post joining to bring him to speed?

3. How long should one wait for the desired performance to be visible (e.g. 2 months post joining or 6 months post joining)?
4. If an employee is not doing well, what corrective actions can be taken?
5. If any new employee resigns, should replacement hiring be done or not?

One would mostly see that many business leaders would be hesitant to answer the above. They would put the onus on Sales HRBPs to figure out the responses to each of these questions and this is where the best opportunity lies for the HRBPs! They need to identify and then propose what is the suitable workforce that needs to be hired based on ground realities and logical metrics mentioned above.

Best way is to define the above metrics and related issues in an objective way and then decide on the additional hiring numbers for the year. If possible, phase-out the big hiring numbers by doing a small pilot for an easier geography/product/customer line and then replicate the success to hire the remaining numbers. But always one should try to keep the new hiring numbers as low as possible.

Alternate ways-

It must be kept in mind that headcount increase is not the only way to increase business performance. There can be many alternate ways to deliver business performance using existing workforce than hiring more employees. Some of them could be-

1. Increasing productivity of existing team members by enhancing their capability, providing resources and tools, empowering decision making.
2. Removing any organization related barriers in delivering performance, e.g., complex work processes, multiple approval levels.
3. Elevating roles to handle bigger responsibilities.
4. Defining proper roles, accountabilities, geographies, targets, customer profiles for existing employees and having robust performance measures to drive them.
5. Removing non-value-added activities.
6. Outsourcing work to other professional agencies rather than hiring employees on company rolls.

Workforce Planning is not only about hiring more people

Workforce Planning is considered an important activity mostly during the stage of business expansion or during the start of a new business year. But it must be acknowledged that workforce planning should be carried out at regular intervals to not only add manpower, but to also evaluate the effectiveness of existing headcount as well as evaluate to let go of a few employees through voluntary retirements or hiring them as part-time retainers. Workforce planning offers an important opportunity to evaluate employee productivity, employee performance and gaps (if any) in delivering business results. The outcome of workforce planning should flow into **'talent management'** initiatives and should result into **'career planning'** for employees to take higher roles or explore different territories based on their performance and potential. Due to this, it is recommended that workforce planning should be done ideally every six months, if not every quarter.

How to do workforce planning?

1. Sales HRBPs should earmark time/weeks in a year and block the schedule of relevant stakeholders involved in the workforce planning.
2. The metrics discussed in previous sections should be well prepared before the discussions
3. It is also essential to connect with key managers to take the inputs from the ground to understand the key issues of performance before the meetings
4. Understand the business KPIs and the planned growth numbers. Understand attrition rate and reasons of attrition.
5. Understand the business goals (if any new sales territories, products or customers will be added).
6. Identify if an increase in manning is actually required to deliver the requisite/desired output.
7. If manning is required, then identify at what level (salesmen or supervisors or managers).
8. Remember if you add more headcount, you also need to add a few employees at the managerial level to maintain the ideal span of control.
9. Create the first proposal yourself along with details on hiring timelines and required resources
10. Highlight any risky areas/legal issues (e.g. in many countries, you can't hire women employees if you are not having a creche facility in the office premises, in other countries you may not be able to hire foreign pass workers unless you maintain the designated local to foreign employee ratio).

Case study:

Michelle recently joined as the Sales HRBP in a financial services company with a large sales force. Her CEO calls her and asks her to hire 10% more sales workforce in the next one month as he projects the sales to growth of 10% this year.

a) What questions can Michelle ask the CEO to get more clarity?
b) How can she present her point of view on hiring?
c) Should she go ahead and hire 10% or push back the CEO?

Summary:

1. Voice of HR on the decision-making table is important, especially during Workforce planning. HR should be involved right from the beginning.

2. HRBPs should build credibility by highlighting the facts, figures and key data from the ground. It is only then that any workforce addition decisions should be made.

3. More people do not always result into better performance. One must find alternative ways to use existing employee strength.

4. Agree with the management on metrics/ KPIs that need to be reviewed if hiring decision is to be made. Review it as per timelines and highlight reasons of deviation.

5. If possible, phase-out the big hiring numbers by doing a small pilot for an easier geography/product/customer line and then replicating the success to hire the remaining numbers. New hiring numbers should be kept as low as possible.

6. The outcome of workforce planning should flow into 'talent management' initiatives and should result into **'career planning'** of employees to take different roles or territories based on their performance and potential.

7. Workforce planning should be carried out at regular intervals, not only to add manpower, but to also evaluate the efficacy of existing headcount.

8. Remember, all organization issues begin with hiring more people than required. Keep the new numbers as low as possible.

Chapter 3: Recruitment & Selection

> *"Development can help great people be even better - but if I had a dollar to spend, I'd spend 70 cents getting the right person in the door."*
> *- Paul Russell*

Often recruitment and selection are used interchangeably, but recruitment is the process of identifying the criteria to hire and then creating awareness amongst the target candidates to apply to the position in the company. Selection is what comes after that, when one actually interviews the potential candidates leading to the offer to join.

An important result of workforce planning is to identify the various roles for which hiring needs to be done and the number of vacancies. In any existing organization, generally the job descriptions ("JD") or role details are already available for various roles. However, often they are dated and do not reflect the actual work that needs to be done. It is important that before proceeding with any recruitment drive, JDs are updated for all the roles in consultation with the hiring managers. They should clearly reflect at least 80% of the responsibilities that the employee should have to perform properly. Along with the JDs, the selection criteria (competencies), selection process and target timelines for the process needs to be decided.

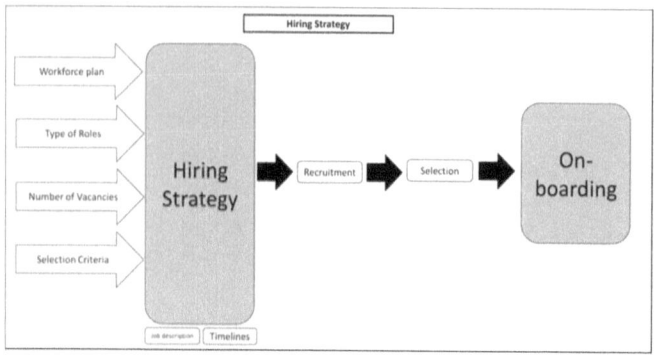

Image I3.1

The image (I3.1) shows the Hiring Strategy for any company for any roles. The output of workforce planning flows into hiring strategy along with other inputs. Output are the details of the recruitment & selection processes followed by employee-on-boarding. Job descriptions and timelines are the two key enablers for deciding the hiring strategy. Hiring budgets, type of payroll (third party or company), inputs from compensation strategy, sources of hiring, are few key elements that need to be decided while formulating a detailed hiring strategy.

One of the best ways to execute any hiring process is to block the calendars of the relevant hiring managers prior to starting the recruitment process for various activities related to hiring (e.g. briefing or pre-placement talks with candidates, interviews, induction and oration.). This ensures that the managers are available during the recruitment and selection process. More importantly, it highlights that this process is important and well planned both to the management and to the applicants.

Selection criteria for various roles

Hiring for any role should be done by identifying the competencies required to execute that role properly. The tables below show the possible competencies that can be used as selection criteria for basic sales roles in any company -

Role	Competency	Definition
Salesmen	Communication skills	Person should be able to communicate his ideas clearly, concisely and in the language preferred by customers. He should be able to use structured communication to present his thoughts and make sales pitch or handle queries/ suggestions.
	Analytical skills	Person should be able to analyze the situation/ market/ customer and accordingly modify his sales pitch to generate sales.
	Quantitative aptitude	Person should be able to do basic math easily. This will help him make profitable pitches to the customer and handle objections by the customer citing data and calculations.
	Ability to generate insights from data	Person should be able to understand/analyze the business drivers and based on existing situation, generate insights to increase

Role	Competency	Definition
Sales Supervisor		business.
	Team management	As several salesmen will report into this position, any person in this role should be able to manage the team in the right and empathetic manner. He should be able to build a team.
	Problem solving	Person should be able to resolve complex customer/ partner/ distributor issues to maintain business continuity. He should be able to identify root cause of any problem and then connect with relevant stakeholders both within and outside the organization.
	Coaching skills	The person should be able to spend considerable time coaching his salesmen on the job. Ability to ask open ended questions, sharing the best practices as well as encouraging the team to learn more will be an important competency.

Table T3.1

Role	Competency	Definition
Sales Managers	Planning skills	Sales managers are often responsible for driving sales for a large territory for multiple products across multiple customers. The person in this role should have planning skills to organize and seek more resources to drive business results.
	Negotiation skills	The person should be able to ideate & propose a mutual win-win solution for the company and the customer. He should be able to prepare for negotiations well by understanding the business context and drivers of the business.
	Influencing skills	The person should be able to influence multiple stakeholders starting with his team to senior management to external customers and partners to drive the business in the right direction.
	Team development skills	The person should be able to train his team using various pedagogy and available resources at regular intervals. He can only succeed if he builds the talent in the team by promoting regular training and developmental activities.

Table T3.2

Ways to drive recruitment process

1. Create or update the JDs for the target roles in consultation with the hiring manager.
2. Identify on whose pay-rolls the hiring will happen. *In many companies, generally, salesmen are hired on distribution partners rolls or on the rolls of Third-party staffing companies to lower employee costs and simplify HR processes. Sales supervisors are either hired on a Third-party staffing companies or on direct payrolls, depending on the hiring strategy of the company. Sales Managers are generally hired on company rolls to ensure better control. This identification process is important to provide absolute clarity to the applicants wrt. who will issue them their offer letter and avoid any surprises in case they are expecting to join on company pay-rolls.*
3. Identify the budgets required to drive the recruitment process and align the management on the cost outlay.
4. It is important to decide on the way one would like to drive the recruitment process. Here are the various strategies:
   a. **Mass hiring of Salesmen/Supervisors through outsourcing/placement agencies**- One can outsource the recruitment process to a professional agency which has contacts on the ground to find relevant candidates and make them aware of the role. These agencies can also help in screening candidates for selection process.
   b. **Online recruitment (Jobsites/Social forums, etc.)**- One can use various

websites specializing in online recruitment. One may need to purchase a license for the same and this might involve costs.

c. **Newspaper ads/posters-** One can post ad on the newspapers/local job posts/magazines as well as make posters and distribute them through the existing employees. One needs to ensure that the local labor laws are followed before this option is opted for.

d. **Using referrals-** Drive a referral program in which the existing employees are made aware of the openings. This is generally the most preferred way as the existing employee can play the role of company's ambassador as well as feel proud if any of their referrals are selected. However, do ensure that the company policies are followed in terms of hiring blood relatives in associate roles.

e. **Ads on trucks/delivery vehicles-** Many companies post their openings on their vehicles/delivery trucks along with a phone number using which the interested candidate may contact.

5. Invite as many applications as you can through this process and screen the applicants basis appropriate selection criteria.

6. Always furnish true and authentic information of the job and the company to the candidates.

Selection Process

This is the tricky part. While many HRBPs feel that this is one of the most important value adding work that HR does in terms of contributing to the growth of the company, often it is not so. This is because while selecting people, especially when you are doing mass hiring for salesmen or supervisors, one needs to effectively take a call in the short 10-15 minutes of interaction with the candidates. From a mere 15-minutes interaction with a candidate, it is very difficult to project how a candidate will behave in real life job situations (which in sales will be mostly unsupervised for long periods of time).

It needs to be made clear to the hiring manager and the management that one can't hire a person who fully matches with the requirement of the role in such a short period of interview time. The sales team often don't want to keep any of their territories vacant for a long period of time and put a demand on the Sales HRBP for quick closures of hiring and onboarding assuming that sales will start booming from the day someone fills in the vacant role. When this doesn't happen because the Sales HRBP cannot always get full 100% match with the requirements, again the buck gets passed to the Sales HRBP.

Setting the right expectations to the stakeholders and partnering with them on the various stages of hiring is the only way one can resolve the above situation. Further, one must look to hire the best-fitting (and not the best) candidates who can then be developed by their respective managers.

Sales HRBPs should also finalize the selection process in terms of who all will interview the candidate and what exact process will be used for the interviews. Ideally, for hiring a salesman, interviews with the distributor partner, sales supervisor and sales manager are sufficient. (HRBP should definitely conduct the first round to screen the candidates). For supervisors, apart from the sales manager, it can be good if the sales director can also interview the person. This ensures sponsorship by the top management as well as highlights that the position is important to the company. The exact process can be decided basis the existing norms in the company with the point that the hiring manager should definitely conduct the interview for the position in his team. This ensures ownership of the candidate as the decision is made by hiring manager as well.

Best way to hire for sales positions

For any frontline sales position, especially for salesmen and sales supervisors, it is important to link back to workforce planning and then plan for hiring the trainees first. Advantage of doing this will be that both the company and the candidate will get time to understand each other well and then take an informed decision in terms of continuing the contract or not. If any of the two parties feel dissatisfied, when the probation/sales trainee period gets over, the relationship can be terminated. The other advantage of doing this will be that time pressure of hiring from the business side can be reduced. Often, one would already have trainees on bench who can join the roles easily.

The above two advantages can drive sustainable business and give more time to the system to train and develop the right talent. This approach is more pro-active than reactive, and business always tends to benefit more with trained resources rather than freshers.

Key points to keep in mind while hiring trainees:

1. Follow the local labor laws before hiring the sales trainees. In many countries, one might need to inform the local employment board and seek potential candidates from them before the positions are opened for external candidates or colleges.

2. While hiring for sales trainees, one must try to hire more employees than the prevailing attrition rate in the company for that role. Example, if the prevailing turnover rate of salesmen in the company is 20%, and that converts into say 100 people, one should target to hire at least 120 trainees at the frontline level. The reason being, there can be attrition at the level of these newly hired sales trainees as well. The company after some time may also feel that the performance of a few individual trainees many not be up to the mark. Hence, one needs to build some cushion of headcount while hiring sales trainees.

3. Build the costs of the Sales Trainee program prior to launching the program. Ensure that all costs relating to recruitment, hiring, onboarding, travelling and other miscellaneous items, are accounted for. Try to keep an option to avail the

first month's salary on the first day of joining by the sales trainees who are asked to relocate from their current cities. This is because many of these candidates (either freshers or experienced) might need cash-in-hand to arrange for accommodation, travel, etc. for the purpose of this job. Business will always be wary of paying upfront to the new sales trainees without them completing a certain time period with the company but extending this benefit will build the trust of the candidates in the company and they will start on a positive note. In case anyone absconds after taking the money, this unfortunate cost will indeed get compensated over time by returns generated by other sales trainees who get confirmed as the quality of candidates will be better. Overall, this will save money as compared to going for relatively costly just-in-time hiring and then finding out the candidate is not good and then repeating the process to find new candidates. Company loses both time and money in this situation.

4. Hire locally for locations where you see most attrition. For sales employees, given their salary range, it is important to hire locally within the reach of their hometowns/current residences. The advantage is that:

    a. These local hires will know their local markets well and hence their ability to promote sales will be better.

    b. They will know the local language and hence can communicate effectively.

    c. Their cost of living expenses will not change much as they can continue staying where they are.

      d. One can confirm the local person in that location itself as the chances of the local person staying with the company will be higher and thereby, reducing the overall attrition rates.

5. While interviewing any candidate for the sales trainee program, try to assess the level of need of the candidate for the job. Understanding the reason is important to ascertain the motivation to join.

6. Have a well-defined onboarding process, company engagement plan and grievance resolution process for these trainees.

7. Communicate very clearly that only the best performers will be confirmed for future roles. All trainees must be paid their stipends/salaries for all the months that they worked in their role as a trainee as per existing norms/labor laws.

Business, many a times may not be willing to fund the sales trainee program as it involves adding further manpower costs. If the turnover rates are not high, or there are limited opportunities for business to expand, one may go for direct hiring rather than launching a sales trainee program. However, for businesses grappling with high turnover or looking at continuous year-on-year growths, the advantages of having the sales trainee program will be much higher than direct hiring.

Key points to keep in mind while hiring sales employees directly from industry:

1. Sales HRBPs should work for a few days with all roles (salesmen/supervisors/managers) across multiple geographies to get a firsthand insight into the nature of these roles. This will help them comprehend the prevalent challenges that the roles face. It will be also help them to understand what can be the necessary selection criteria to ensure success in these roles.
2. Have a well-defined selection criteria and interview process while hiring sales employees.
3. The selection process should be communicated well in advance to the candidates (e.g. how many interview rounds will be conducted, nature of group activities, etc.) so that the candidates can prepare in advance and plan for the day.
4. Ensure to onboard the hiring managers/selection team on the tools being planned to be used for the selection process (competencies, interview questions, etc.).
5. The selection process should be tailored around the competencies to be checked for the role.
6. Ensure that the candidate is willing to travel as most of the sales roles in many companies require flexibility in travel.
7. A few tips on the selection tools-
    a. Ensure to have appropriate selection tools to check for proficiency in spoken and written language (both the language preferred by customers and the language in which company communications are done).

    b. During the selection process, observe the behavior of the candidate both under conditions in which he/she needs to behave individually (e.g. interview or responding to questionnaire, etc.) as well as where they participate with others (e.g. group discussions, group activities, etc.). This is because sales have to be done using both individual personalities, and social interactions. Ability to influence others using on the feet thinking as well as displaying positive group behavior are traits required for all the roles in Sales.

8. Relevant experiences of the role in similar organizations can be an added advantage as the candidate may already know about the sales processes, markets, customers etc. and can get onboarded faster. However, do check for the company's policy on hiring from competitors before resorting to this step. Also, ensure whether the candidate has signed a no-poaching/non-compete agreement or a bond with the previous company which can restrict his/her employment.

9. If any hiring consultant or an external search agency are involved, ensure to have a valid agreement on the terms of the payment on availing their services.

10. It is also a good practice to have a retention clause included with external agencies. (Retention clause means that if the recommended candidate leaves within 3 or 6 months of joining, the hiring consultant needs to refund the fees or provide alternate candidate(s)).

Key Points to keep in mind while hiring sales employees through referrals

1. Ensure the referral program is communicated properly to all existing employees.
2. Market the referral programs effectively and make it an important hiring avenue.
3. Build a small monetary award for the employees in case their referrals get selected.
4. Ensure that the employees are encouraged to reveal the actual relationship with the candidates they are referring. This is sometimes important as one may not want conflict of interest issues or hand-in-gloves issues (brother being hired as a direct reportee, husband and wife working in the same department, similar to conflicting roles etc.).

As you see, hiring is a complex process and needs collaboration with various stakeholders inside and outside the organization. Hiring KPIs like successful hiring ratio (no. of candidates who are finalized by no. of applicants) time to first interview, time to on-board, etc. can make the process objective for the Sales HRBP and business.

A pro-active and well-defined hiring strategy can set both the company and the new employees on a path to success.

Case Study:

Ralston is working as a Sales HRBP for a FMCG company which is witnessing turnover of sales supervisors at the rate of 40% in the last two years. The business is under pressure as sales targets are not getting delivered due to high attrition. The Sales Director blames this situation to the hiring of candidates with a wrong profile due to a high pressure to hire the candidates quickly.

a) What can Ralston do to understand this situation better?

b) Should he continue with the existing hiring norms? If not, what all aspects should he include as part of shortlisting and hiring criteria?

c) How can he define a successful hiring strategy?

Summary:

1. Recruitment is the process of identifying the criteria to hire and then to create awareness amongst the target candidates to apply to the vacancy in the company. Selection is what follows after that- when one actually interviews the candidates and gives the best fit candidate the offer to join.

2. It is always important that before HRBPs proceed with recruitment, they finalize the JDs of the roles in consultation with the hiring managers. The JDs should clearly cover at least 80% of the work that the role should do.

3. It needs to be made clear to the hiring manager and the management that one cannot hire a person who fully matches with the requirement of the role in short periods of interview process.

4. For any frontline sales position, especially for salesmen and sales supervisors, it is important to link back to workforce planning and then plan for hiring 'Sales Trainees' first.

5. While hiring for sales trainees, try to hire more people than the prevailing attrition rate in the company.

6. Hire locally for locations where you see the most attrition. For sales employees, given their salary range, it is important to hire locally within the reach of their hometowns/current residences.

7. The selection process should be tailored around the competencies one needs to have for that role.

8. Identify the level of need of the candidate for looking for a job. It is important to understand the reason to ascertain the motivation to join.

Blank Page

Chapter 4: On-Boarding

> *"I truly believe that onboarding is an art. Each new employee brings with them a potential to achieve and succeed. To lose the energy of a new hire through poor onboarding is an opportunity lost."*
>
> *- Sarah Wetzel*

This is perhaps the most neglected HR process, given that the business wants to fill up the vacant position in the fastest way possible and devoting time for on-boarding is difficult. However, often, this is the most important step from the perspective of a new employee and gives him a clear impression of the company's approach towards its employees.

The best on-boarding plan has the right structure, interventions and schedule to on-board and induct any sales employee smoothly. All documentations of the new employee should be mandatorily taken as per the company procedure and prevailing labor laws. Ensuring an employee file is created either in hard copy or online is essential. A good practice of this age is to have an online documentation process that a new employee can access even before his joining. This saves his crucial time on the first day and he can focus more on meeting important stakeholders than on paperwork.

Ideally, onboarding for the sales employees should cover the following topics so that the employee can understand the role, organization & ways of working easily-

Salesman:

1. All products and services.
2. Sales pitch for products/product benefits.
3. Price of the products.
4. Margins available to various stakeholders in distribution value chain.
5. Basic manufacturing process of the product or service details (how the service is delivered).
6. How to calculate selling price/discounting, etc.
7. If any sales automation device is to be used to make sales, a full demo should be included.
8. Basics of distributor/partner operations.
9. How the payment process will be run.
10. Basic objection handling process of the customers.
11. How to sell, how to sell more, how to pitch to new customers, execution of products inside a store.
12. Salary and incentive structure and the payroll the new employee is in (Partner, Third party staffing agency or company).
13. Introduction to various stakeholders- supervisor, distributor owner, distributor manager, key customers, delivery agent, product servicing team etc.
14. Company's guidelines on ethics and values.

Sales Supervisors:

1. All of the above.
2. Details of distributor/partner operations.
3. Training/coaching materials for self and the team. (Best practice is to have online onboarding programs to cover for these topics).
4. Details of Sales processes of the company.
5. Interaction with supply chain, finance, HR, sales managers, sales head, etc.
6. Grievance resolution mechanism.
7. Key business levers to drive sales and execution in the market.

Sales Managers:

1. All of the above.
2. Detailed sales & distribution processes.
3. Key stakeholders- function heads, distributor/partners, vendors, etc.
4. Details of all training materials (offline and online).
5. Details of product, pricing, discounting, profits levers, etc.
6. Full introduction of all team members, their tenure, experiences, high performers, concerns, their developmental inputs, etc.
7. Any pending issues/legal disputes, etc.

While onboarding any of the sales employees, the following actions might help:

1. Ensure that any onboarding day is kept as long as the general working hours of any other employee in that role. (Keeping onboarding days light and short might give a wrong impression that the company is easy going and vice versa). The onboarding plan should reflect the average existing work pressure and habits of people in that role.

2. Ensure that the new joiners' bank account numbers, tax proofs, etc. are properly registered in the system. It is often seen, especially at the level of salesman that the name they mention on the employee form (many times their nick-names) and the actual name mentioned in their bank account is different. If the cheques are issued based on the nick-name mentioned in the employee form, after a month of hard work, it will not get processed in the bank account resulting into employee grievances and issues. Further, account numbers need to be registered in the payroll servers properly after cross-checking with a proof issued by the bank (e.g.- cheque book, bank statement, etc.). Even a one-digit manual error in 10 to 20 digits bank account number can cause delays in first salary payment, leaving a bad taste in the employee's mind.

3. At the end of the on-boarding, an opportunity should be given to any new joiner to answer a quiz of the topics he had been introduced as part of on-boarding. This will indicate the quality of the on-boarding program as well as the learning of the new employee. It should be communicated to the employee that he will have to appear for this

particular quiz on the first day on-boarding so that he is attentive and tries to learn as much as he can. (Don't use this quiz to reward or punish the new employee as this is not the purpose of this quiz).

4. There should be a feedback and an evaluation form at the end of onboarding session which the employee should fill up anonymously. This ensures if they have any feedback to share, they can share it without any repercussions or identifications.

5. As mentioned for the section on 'Sales Trainees' before, it is important to keep an option of paying the first month's salary upfront if the candidate is joining in a location which is not his current residence. This will increase the trust of the employees in the company.

6. As much as possible, onboarding process should be made online so that the employee can focus more on interaction with critical stakeholders during the first few days of joining rather than spending it on paperwork or online trainings.

It should be noted that while the designing of the onboarding plan is the responsibility of HR, execution of the plan remains first with the manager and then with the HR. **A proper onboarding can ensure good first impressions in the mind of any new employee and can encourage him to put his best for the company.**

Case Study:

XYZ company is in a start-up phase. They are planning to hire over 100 sales team members over the next two months. Jaine is working as the HRBP in this startup.

a) How should Jaine create a solid onboarding plan for all new joiners?

b) What can she do to accelerate the learning of the new joiners so that they can start impacting sales quickly?

c) Should she propose an online on-boarding plan or an offline plan?

Summary:

1. On-boarding is the most important step from the perspective of a new employee and gives him a clear sneak peek of the company's approach towards its employees.

2. A good practice is to have an online documentation process which a new employee can access even before his joining. This saves his crucial time when he joins on the first day and he can focus more on meeting important stakeholders than on paperwork.

3. There should be a quiz, a feedback and an evaluation form at the end of onboarding which the new employee should attend.

On-Boarding

> *CXO - What if we train our employees and they leave?*
> *CEO- What if we don't.......and they stay?*
> *- a common internet joke*

Capability building is one of the most important but severely under-rated HR process in many organizations. Most organizations are interested to hire sales employees, but they are not ready to allow their sales employees to take time out of their daily routines to build their own and their team's capability. But if one doesn't sharpen the axe regularly, how can one deliver better performance?

Many good organizations have realized the importance of this vertical and have a dedicated function- **Sales Capability** to have targeted capability interventions for their sales teams. The role of the sales capability managers is to ensure focused training of all the sales employees across the organization.

Formulating a Sales Capability Strategy

Building 'Sales Capability Strategy' needs inputs from multiple stakeholders and requires extensive work which is beyond the scope of this book. However, at its simplest level, image (I5.1) best defines the elements of 'Sales Capability Strategy.'

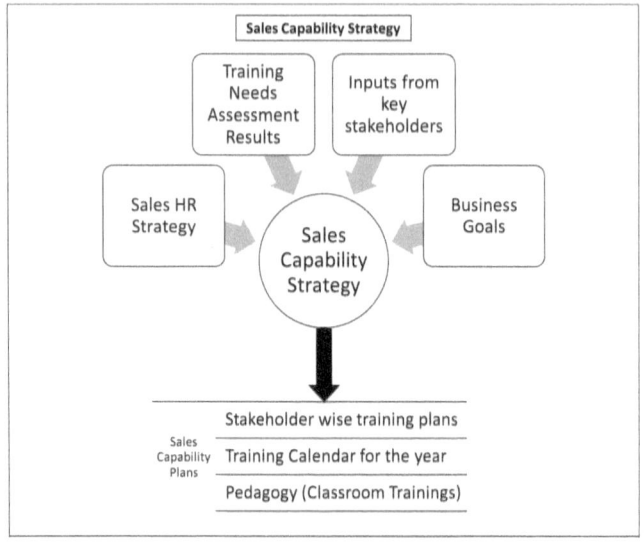

Image I5.1

Elements of Sales Capability Strategy

In order to formulate an effective Sales Capability Strategy, it is important to first understand the overall Sales HR Strategy, conduct a 'training needs assessment' for various sales roles, take inputs from relevant stakeholders & understand business goals in details.

All the above inputs will need to be categorized into short-term, medium-term and long-term aspects. Then, a detailed analysis should be done on whether the issues can be resolved by conducting training or requires other interventions. In many situations, training is not the only solution for resolving the business challenge.

If it comes out that training is the most effective solution to these business issues, then a logical 'training plan' needs to be prepared for each stakeholder. Selecting only one topic and training all roles within the sales function in that topic may not be the ideal solution. It is important to analyze the degree of performance gap that exists in each role before creating or borrowing the content for conducting training.

'Training needs identification' is the most important first step and sufficient time and resources should be spent to create a holistic and effective training plan that addresses these needs. The outcome of all these should be the specific training topics for different stakeholders, a training calendar and identification of the right pedagogy to deploy for the training.

Time is of importance for the sales employees

An important aspect that needs to be considered while creating a Sales Capability Strategy is that the time available for training is limited. An important complexity can also include the fact that the sales employees are geographically spread across many locations, may speak and understand only regional local language, timings of work can vary depending on locations and customer they are servicing and may have limited accessibility to training materials and/or internet. All these add to the main constraint of time availability for trainings. If they are pressurized to attend trainings in midst of an urgent business work, they might comply because the company is organizing the training, but they will not be receptive to learning.

Capability initiatives for sales employees need to be short in duration, easy to learn, encourage employees to apply the learnings to their role and should ideally be in the language that the sales employees are adept in. Further, all such planned interventions/ trainings should be repeated at regular intervals to encourage repeat learning and retention. The learning initiatives should also give an opportunity to the team to understand practical application of the learning in a safe environment (e.g. role plays, etc.) so that they can build confidence.

Formulating sales capability plans for Salesmen

1. The HRBP or Capability manager should ideally work in the market with a cross-section of salesmen talent (high-performing, low-performing, serving different customer types, new hire, experienced, etc.) in different geographies to understand the intricacies involved in each role.
2. On-the-job coaching is the best way to train any salesmen. Sufficient processes should be made to encourage regular on the job coaching for all salesmen.
3. For trainings, the learning content for salesmen should be short, precise, focused on key concepts and easily implementable. There should be opportunities in the learning program to encourage the salesmen to practice (through role-plays, simulations etc.) the concepts they have learnt.
4. The learning content should preferably be in the local language of the salesmen to ensure he is able to learn the concepts easily. In case this is not possible, then at least for power-point

presentations and video training content, subtitles should be provided in local language.

5. If a trainer is being used, he/she should be able to converse in local language to clarify all queries.

6. The learning content should be very simple and not focus on more than 2-3 concepts in one module.

7. For salesmen, as the market time is more important, any capability interventions should be planned post market hours. (A few organizations practice repeated learning sessions of 15-30 mins in morning or evening, either every day or once in a week).

8. Impactful learning content for salesmen are in small video bites, also known as 'micro-learning videos'. The advantage of having the learning program through learning videos are:

   a. Micro-learning videos are currently the most popular way of learning. (Most of us spend good time on social media platforms and the growth of micro-videos is easy to observe).

   b. Videos, as a learning material, can be accessed easily at any point in time convenient to the salesperson.

   c. Videos are best way easy to gain attention for both auditory and visual learners.

   d. The learning can be repeated by watching videos again and again.

   e. The content of the videos does not get diluted during distribution of learning across multiple roles. (This is not true for power-point based learning, where each facilitator adds his understanding of the concepts during presentation).

f.   Learning videos can be easily translated into local languages.

g.   The videos can be shared across multiple geographies over the internet.

h.   Videos, once made, can be used regularly to even on-board new joiners.

i.   Videos can be easily made using a mobile phone and a basic video editor. Professionals can also be hired for making them (if budgets permit).

j.   Videos can be supplemented by explanation of topics in further details by supervisors in a classroom setting. This is called an 'assisted video learning' wherein supervisors can add their local experiences as well as resolve any query from salesmen.

Formulating sales capability plans for supervisors

1.   Supervisors will need training on business topics which are more specific to their needs and hence identifying their training needs in detail is very important.

2.   Supervisors, like salesmen can be posted across multiple geographies and hence micro-learning videos can be effective for them as well.

3.   Apart from functional skills, supervisors also need to be trained on facilitation skills so that whatever they learn, they can cascade to their teams easily and effectively.

4.   Best training method for supervisors is classroom training. Due to their geographic spread, virtual classroom trainings can also be used. However,

virtual training should not be planned for an entire day as participants can get distracted after a certain amount of time and keeping their focus on training can be difficult.

Few tips to ensure effective virtual trainings

1. Each virtual training session should be only about 3-4 hours long during any day.
2. A virtual training should be planned for 2 sessions of 90 minutes each with a break in between.
3. In each session, after every 20 minutes, there should be an activity, quiz, online discussion in virtual rooms, etc. as the ability of active listening reduces post 20 mins.
4. Multiple choice questions on the topic that ran in the last 20 minutes can be a great engagement tool as participants can respond using the chat-box and the trainer can assess the -
    a. Depth of understanding on the topic.
    b. Participations level of the audience.
5. Training video(s) should not be used frequently during a virtual training as it consumes bandwidth and the participants may not be able to hear the audio or see the fonts in the video properly. Best way to share these videos is to send them over a link as a pre-read before the virtual session.
6. It is advisable to keep the video of the participants on during any virtual session so that the presenter is able to gauge the body language and the interest of the audience and accordingly modify his presentation/tonality of voice. Participants also remain conscious that if they keep their video on, they have to be attentive. However, if there are

many participants (>100) and internet speed is limited, videos can be turned off to save bandwidth and ensure clarity of communication from the presenter.

Formulating sales capability plans for sales managers

Trainings for sales managers need to be thorough and detailed to touch on all the aspects identified during the 'training needs assessment'. Further, training for sales manager should also focus on building key sales competencies that will result into enhanced performance over medium to short term period.

Best way to train sales managers is to organize classroom trainings. There is no other method (virtual training/videos, etc.) that can be as effective as classroom training for sales managers. As the role of sales managers is very important and a large percentage of their work also involves coaching, influencing and training their own team members, it is important to have a focused training strategy for all sales managers.

It is important to include simulation, case studies, role-plays as practice sessions in all trainings for sales managers. This will ensure that they can learn how to implement their learnings in their daily life as well as further conduct the training for their teams. Virtual and online trainings can be used as refresher trainings for the classroom training topics that have been presented before.

Training Evaluation

Every sales leader is interested to know how will the training initiatives get evaluated? Will there be an objective process of evaluating whether the time spent on training will impact company's goals positively or not? This is in fact the most difficult question to answer for any Learning & Development ("L&D") or capability professionals or HRBPs and hence, the best way to resolve this is to build training evaluation plan as part of the training plan itself.

There are several models for conducting training evaluation, but the following ones are easy to implement:

1. **Kirkpatrick's Four Level of training evaluation.**
2. **Jack Philips ROI model.**

It must be noted that the ability to implement the above models to all levels of evaluation depend on the resources provided to the sales capability team as many of the levels need to be measured continuously over a period of time and might need more hands on the deck. With technology coming to rescue and tools like 'survey monkey' or 'Google forms' becoming available to everyone, training evaluation can be implemented a bit easily.

The output of the training evaluation should be shared with the team and any feedback for improvement must be quickly worked on. Also, not all trainings can be measures for all levels. A few behavioral trainings like team management skills and coaching skills can have objective criteria of measurement but may not have impact on all the levels of evaluations like ROI (return on investment).

With increased focus on productivity, the sales capability team must include training evaluation for all the initiatives they are launching for all roles. This provides a window of opportunity to learn the business as well as objectively measure the impact of the efforts made for training. **A well-trained sales team provides huge advantage to any business in the market.**

Case Study:

A Malaysian Chocolate selling company wants to create a Sales Capability Roadmap for the next 3 years to train all their 1000 salesmen, 450 supervisors and 90 sales managers. They are in a highly competitive environment and with the advent of the ride hailing bikes and taxis, they are facing high attrition of the salesmen due to salary issues. Sam is working as the Sales Capability Manager in this company-

a) What factors should Sam consider while building a Sales Capability Strategy for the team for 3 years?

b) What questions he might need to ask business to get more information for building the sales capability plans?

c) Can he in any manner impact the attrition of salesmen or should he leave it to the compensation team to address this situation?

Summary:

1. Sharpening the axe through regular and repeated trainings is important to ensure that the sales team build their skills & execute in the market in the right manner.

2. Sales capability is perhaps one the most important HR process and it is recommended to have a dedicated team to drive this function.

3. Sales HR Strategy, training needs assessment for various roles, inputs from relevant stakeholders and understanding business goals are key inputs for building a robust Sales Capability Strategy

4. A detailed analysis should be done on whether the sales performance issues can be resolved by conducting training or requires other interventions. In many situations, training may not be the only solution for resolving the business challenge.

5. 'Training needs identification' is the most important first step and sufficient time and resources should be spent/ invested to create a holistic and effective training plan that addresses these needs.

6. Capability initiatives for sales employees need to be short in duration, easy to learn, encourage employees to apply the learnings to their role and should ideally be in the language in which the sales employees are affluent.

7. Micro learning videos are one of the most effective ways to reach to the salesmen. Virtual trainings for sales supervisors and classroom trainings for managers are advisable for effective trainings.

8. With increased focus on productivity, the sales capability team must include training evaluation for all the initiatives they are launching for all roles.

Chapter 6: Talent Management-
Performance & Careers

> *"You cannot push anyone up the ladder unless they are willing to climb." – Andrew Carnegie*

'Talent management strategy' for the sales team is required to ensure that there is a structured way to develop, motivate, retain as well as build careers of the sales team members. While talent management strategy is meant to include all the major HR processes, the scope of this chapter is limited to the relatively important ones –

1. Performance Management.
2. Career Management.

Performance Management-

Sales is one of the easiest functions to set and track performance measures as there is wide availability of hard data like sales numbers, revenue growth, share gain, etc. Issues arise while one is setting the objectives for the softer skills like team management, customer management, displaying right behavior towards customer and team, taking sustainable decisions, etc. and that's where the crux lies.

Each sales person thinks that if he/she can achieve the sales numbers, he/she is set for a fast career growth. But it is well known that is an excellent salesman may not become an excellent sales manager. While sales numbers do matter and people with consistent results are looked at for the higher responsibilities, inability of the person to be flexible to learn the softer people aspects, as well as inability of the organization to support this role transition often leads to disaster for the employee and the organization. Hence, performance management should include these aspects right from the beginning rather than reserving it for only the top roles.

Performance Management for Salesmen

1. The performance management system for salesmen should be designed in such a way that it should be simple to explain to as well as simple to understand by any salesman.
2. Not more than 5 key performance indicators ("KPIs") should be used for target setting, review and performance appraisals.
3. Hard data such as sales (revenue or pieces of weight/volume, etc.), as well as key productivity KPIs (like output per outlet or route or customer, range sold, etc.) can be looked as the main KPIs.
4. Customer feedback should always be a part of the KPIs as behavior of the salesmen can only be gauged by the customer. This is one of the most important soft KPIs to be included to ensure that right behavior is displayed by the salesmen at all times as well sustainable business is assured.

5. Review of KPIs should be done on a periodic basis. In many companies it is done during the daily morning meeting with the supervisor.

6. Performance feedback should be given to the salesmen regularly rather than waiting for one or two opportune moments during the year. The best time to give feedback is when the supervisor has actually worked with the salesmen in the market and seen his performance first hand.

7. Annual increments should be offered considering the local government regulations as well as overall performance delivered on various KPIs.

8. Incentives for salesmen should help drive the main input and output KPIs rather than driving basic employment related issues like attendance, duration of work, etc.

Performance management for supervisors & managers

Performance management for supervisors and managers must be more detailed, periodic and apart from hard sales data, it should cover softer aspects like:

1. Performance on team management.
2. Coaching/training KPIs.
3. Feedback from team members.
4. Overall customers and partner's feedback.

The reason for selecting such aspects is that the roles of the supervisors and managers are not only meant to drive the short-term performance in terms of sales numbers but also to build the right people skills for sustainable business. Further, these KPIs are important from the career growth perspective as well. Any supervisor can only become a manager only when he has shown superior team management skills.

Performance management cycle

Generally, performance management is carried out in a cyclical manner although many organizations are moving towards real-time performance management. Both have their own advantages and disadvantages, but essential thing is to provide clarity to the team members on what their role is and what they need achieve in the given time which can be measured regularly.

The other important thing is to have periodic reviews to understand if the actions are in the right direction to the get the desired results or not. As sales is ultimately a team effort, just having the right pricing, discounting, product, etc. may not always result into the desired results. It is the actions of people that drive results. Ensuring people are focused on right priorities, identifying any performance gaps through regular reviews and giving a construct feedback is of utmost importance.

Image I6.1

The performance management cycle starts with objective setting where the team member sets the goals for the year (refer Image I6.1). There are various ways for setting the objectives in a simple manner, e.g. SMART[1], MBO[2], balance scorecard, etc. The objectives should be stretched but achievable and should motivate the employee to learn and achieve more. The next stage of the cycle is to do the periodic reviews, monthly, quarterly or half yearly. In many organizations, the reviews are done whenever required rather than a periodic setting. The next stage is the 'end year review or annual review'. The final stage is the full

---

[1] Specific, Measurable, Achievable, Relevant, Time bound
[2] Management by objectives

year performance discussions on what went well and what couldn't.

How to deal with poor performers

There will be cases of poor performers in sales. It needs to be ascertained to what extent was poor performance due to external factors which was beyond the control of the person in that role, and what wasn't. If one can satisfactorily conclude that the poor performance was more because of the actions or inactions of the person involved, right processes need to be set and adhered to handle such situations, rather than blindly firing that person. Hiring and firing without due diligence can lead to employee demotivation, litigation and dis-repute to the organization.

It is important to have a well-defined process to plan improvement measures through tasking, etc. The logical way can be as follows:

1. Understand if there are any legalities involved to treat such a situation (e.g. probation period, mandatory local hiring norms, etc.).
2. Understand how the peer companies are dealing with such situations.
3. It is always advisable that hiring and firing should be done delicately and with sufficient evidences that can help in proving the direness of the situation to anyone.
4. Set out a process to first inform the person of what has led to poor performance and what could have been done alternatively to avoid the situation. Give

enough time and inputs to the employee to work on his development and then do things in a right way.

5. Give clear timelines on how long the process will last and how it will be reviewed, against which objectives. Also, clearly communicate what the possible outcomes can be, which in this case may be:
   a. Continuation in current role as performance gaps are addressed.
   b. Extension of above review period to give another chance as gaps exist, but considerable efforts from the employee can be observed to address the situation.
   c. Separation/termination in case this process does not result in change of behavior.
6. It is important to keep sufficient records of such processes as any employment terms may be contended in courts as per local laws.
7. Separation, if the case so requires, should be done professionally without hurting the sentiments or disparaging the individual.
8. Ideally, an outplacement service should be provided to facilitate the movement of the employee outside the organization to ensure his livelihood continues.

Career management

The internal drive of sales employees to grow the business is proportional to their own drive to grow further in their careers. Having a structured 'career management process' is important to ensure the aspirations of career growth are managed in a transparent way for the sales employees. This also builds the motivation of the sales employees to perform better and strengthens the sales employees' trust in the company and the management.

For any company, the roles and hierarchy of roles in sales must be clearly defined in order to provide clarity of career growths options. This should also include those roles which are support roles for sales, and require extensive knowledge of sales processes, like, sales IT management, market execution, sales capability, trade marketing, etc. Many companies have career growth plans designed in such a way that doing a sales support role is important and mandatory for growth in subsequent sales roles. This ensures that the employees get exposure to different parts of the business and are cognizant of the importance of all roles.

Career progression should be based on:

1. Consistent delivery of business results in current role.
2. Potential to grow.
3. Availability of vacant roles.
4. Understanding the levers of business, including people management.

For a sales employee, any career decision can be looked from the lens of the 4L Model. Organizations also need to configure the career strategy which helps in answering the 4Ls- Level, Learning, location and Life stage (Image I6.2).

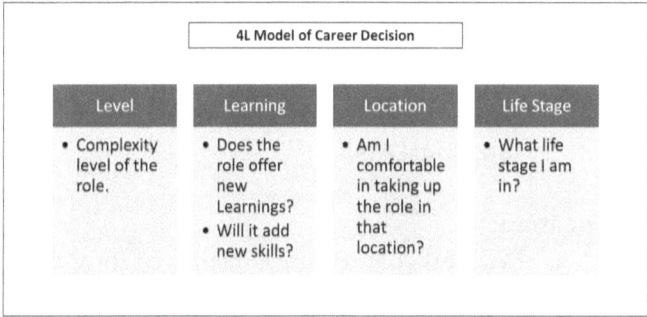

Image I6.2

As a Sales HRBP, if one wants to attract the right talent for any of the roles, one will need to answer the above 4Ls for the employee:

1. **Level (of complexity):**
   a. What is the level of difficulty in the role?
   b. Is it relatively a simpler role or a complex role compared to the existing one which the employee is doing?
   c. Does it appear as a natural progression of the current role or is it a totally different stream?
   d. Will it lead to a growth in salary and incentive?

2. Learning:

    a. What new learnings does the role offer?

    b. Will these learnings help the employee take bigger roles in his/her career in the future?

    c. Is this a differentiated learning experience (e.g. moving from core sales to sales support) or an extension of existing role with increased span?

    d. Does it offer a mix of both generalist skills (like team management, etc.) and functional skills?

3. Location:

    a. Will this role require a change of location?

    b. Is the location better depending on the employee's current location or not (e.g. moving from a city location to sub-urban or moving from the HQ location to a regional office location, etc.).

    c. Will it be feasible for the employee's family to move in the new location?

4. Life Stage:

    a. In what life stage is the employee currently in? Is he/she a bachelor(change this term) or about to get married? Is the spouse working? At what school level (change to stage of education) are his children in?

    b. How far is the hometown of the employee?

    c. Is the employee an experienced employee or a new employee in the company?

    d. Overall, is the employee ready for the change with respect to aspects like family, etc. and will this change be sustainable for the employee and the family.

Basis the answers to above 4Ls, one can design the career strategy as well as encourage sales employees to apply for internal roles.

An important aspect of career management is to also give the visibility of the average time that it might take for an employee to move to different roles. Depending on the size of the company and internal hierarchy, this time should be communicated properly to all the employees and the expectations should be set in a transparent manner. It is also important to explain how employees can limit their own career growth if they are fixed on specific roles, locations or time of change.

Career management for salesmen

Salesmen generally form one of the largest headcounts in any company and managing their careers is generally limited as they are on third-party staffing company's rolls or on a Partner's role. However, they still have expectations of career growth and ambition to take higher roles like that of sales supervisors and managers and fairly so.

It is important to have a career management strategy for salesmen, given they are the face of the company and keeping them associated with the company for a long term is more beneficial to the company. The following points can be considered to design a career management strategy for salesmen:

1. Transition from salesmen to supervisor roles are at

times guided by local labor laws. They must be referred and adhered to while designing the strategy.

2. Location plays a very important factor for salesmen aspiring for supervisor roles. Language is also an important consideration. Not all salesmen are locationally mobile. Any career management plan should incorporate this important factor. Ideally, roles should be offered to salesmen within 100 kms of their existing location where variance of language is low, and the salesmen can travel back to the hometown on weekends/monthly.

3. Criteria for application to supervisor roles should be fixed and well communicated. A few of them may include:

   a. Minimum tenure completion as a salesman.
   b. Cut-off for sales performance.
   c. Ability to converse in local language and official language followed in the company.
   d. Absence of any disciplinary proceedings.
   e. Demonstrated ability to adopt new practices (may be digital, team management skills, presentation skills, etc.).

Career management for supervisors & managers

In Sales, establishing relationship with customers is the key. For this, any supervisor or manager need to spend sufficient time in his domain/territory to understand the products, levers of business and customer behavior in details. However, it is equally important to experience different channels, geographies, product verticals to grow in the sales career. A few important aspects of managing careers for supervisors and managers are as follows:

1. The supervisors and managers should spend at least two years in the role that they have joined to understand the business environment, be productive and learn about business. The logic behind this is that it takes around first 90 days to get inducted into the territory or profile, the next 180 days to identify business levers, challenges & issues, key stakeholders, the next 90-180 days to align systems and process to drive performance and the next 1 year to repeat the above cycle and deliver superior results.

2. While it makes sense for them to continue as long as in the role, but there are business risks of keeping sales employees in one territory for a long time. It is also not prudent for an employee to master only one aspect of business by staying in one role/territory for a long time. Career Management strategy for the supervisors and managers should build in options for team member to apply for different roles within the organization to get differentiated experiences and grow in their careers.

3. These movements should not only be restricted to sales function or allied functions likes Sales IT, Trade marketing, customer service, etc. it should have options to explore other functions like finance, HR, operations, supply chain, etc.

4. Sales HRBP will need to establish a process of posting vacancies in the company which are visible to all employees. Processes will also need to be made to define the criteria of eligibility for internal

employees, how they can apply for these positions and the selection criteria.

5. It is very important to use the interview process to also give developmental feedback to those internal candidates who have not been selected for a particular role. Absence of this can create a sense of mistrust in the process and create grievances.

6. Basis the 'Talent Landscape' (see the chapter on Attrition or turnover management), a pipeline of talent can be created for critical roles and relevant employees can be groomed to take up higher roles as part of talent succession plan.

Innovative career management strategies

In many situations, Sales HRBPs can adopt the following innovative career management strategies-

1. **Externships**

   There are numerous vendors, partners, allied companies, agencies, etc. that each of the company works. Sales HRBPs can create short, relevant and on exchange basis career opportunities for the sales employees by adopting 'Externships'. Externships are occasions in which you can ask your employee to go and work on a project in any of the other companies to learn from their best practices. In return, you also offer externships to the partner organizations to send their employees to your company and learn from your best practices. This practice will of course require management buy-in and sponsorship but can be justified by the value addition it will do the company and to the employees.

2. Shadow Stints

The chosen sales employees can be encouraged to shadow the current incumbent of the senior role they are targeting as their next move. This will give immense opportunities to the sales employee to understand the role in detail so that he can take an informed call when the vacancy comes in the future. This will also help the employee gain more confidence and help him acquire the necessary skills needed for the next job.

3. Projects

Projects offer great opportunity for employees to work with different employees and understand the way they operate as well as build networks within the organization. This also gives the employees to build more skills. Projects should be made in such a way that it benefits the organization along with benefitting the participating employees.

Conclusion

As you see, Talent Management is an important HR process in any organization. **It can provide a reason for the employees to give their best and stay committed to the objectives of the organization.**

Case Study:

Vinh is a good performer but is stuck in the role of a sales supervisor for the past 4 years. He has been eyeing the role of the area sales manager in a different customer vertical for the past few months and had also approached his manager and HRBP, however, things don't seem to be moving.

a) Is there a risk that Vinh might attrite?
b) What can Vinh do to get the role he desires?
c) How can HRBP support him to achieve his career goals?

Summary:

1. Sales is one of the easiest functions to set and track performance measures as there is wide availability of hard data like sales numbers, revenue growth, share gain, etc.

2. While sales numbers do matter and people with consistent results are looked for next level role, inability of the person to be flexible to learn the softer people aspects, as well as inability of the organization to build relevant skills in this role transition often leads to disaster for the employee.

3. Ensuring people are focused on right priorities and identifying any performance gaps through regular reviews and giving a construct feedback is of utmost importance.

4. There will be cases of poor performers. It needs to be ascertained to what extent was the impact on performance due to external factors which was beyond the control of the person in the role and which weren't. Any tasking given to poor performer should be kept confidential to preserve the respect of the employee.

5. Career Strategy for employees as well as career choices depend on 4Ls- Level, Location, Learning & Life Stage.

6. It is important to have a career management strategy for salesmen, given they are the face of the company and keeping them associated with the company for a long term is more beneficial to the company.

7. Location plays a very important factor for salesmen aspiring for supervisor roles. Language is also an important consideration. Not all salesmen are locationally mobile.

8. Sales HRBP will need to establish a process of posting vacancies in the company which are visible to all employees.
9. The supervisors and managers should spend at least two years in the role that they have joined to understand the business environment, be productive and learn about business.
10. Externships are occasions in which you can ask your employee to go and work with any of the other companies to learn from their best practices. In return, you also offer externships to the partner organization's employees to come to your company and learn your best practices.

Chapter 7: Employee Engagement & Motivation

> *"In order to build a rewarding employee experience, you need to understand what matters most to your people."* –
> *Julie Bevacqua*

Employee engagement is a way to have a series of year-long initiatives to keep the sales team occupied in a constructive way that keeps them motivated and increases the bonding with the company. Having a well-defined engagement strategy for the sales team not only improves the commitment of the team, but also leads to higher retention of talent.

Best employee engagement initiatives are those which are planned, designed, participated, performed and measured by the sales team themselves. With a great sales talent pool, one will find a number of singers, artists, comedians, musicians, poets, sportspersons, quizmasters, etc. in the team. A good engagement strategy is to identify these hobbyists and encourage them and others to display their talent to the larger audience in the company.

A few engagement initiatives that work well without involving much budgets include:

1. Online and offline quiz contests (on general topics as well as company related topics).
2. Gamified learning initiatives.
3. Initiatives like – 'Company has got talent' (replica of America has got talent, etc.).
4. Family day celebrations.
5. New year celebrations with family.
6. Weekly and monthly online and offline game tournaments.
7. Sports tournament.
8. Festival celebrations.
9. Informal team gatherings.
10. Team excursions.
11. Factory/farm/site visits.
12. Attending any live sports matches with team.

It is generally suggested that the Sales HRBPs can look at partnering with various sales team members to create communities of practice or 'task-force' teams who can identify the engagement initiatives and roll-them out to the larger audience. It also works well if a new joiner is given a choice to join any of such teams right at the time of his joining. Each of these teams should present their thoughts and ideas to the management and seek the necessary resources to run them. It is important to phase all these engagement activities round the year so that the larger team is engaged throughout

Engagement with the employee's family

Family forms an important aspect of an employee's life. With sales employees travelling for multiple days and inadvertently staying away from family members, there should always be engagement programs planned around family members. This helps form a strong bond of the family with the company and creates a significant positive impact in the mind of the employees and increases their commitment towards work. Again, inputs must be taken from the team on what they believe can be the best way to engage with families depending on local culture and practices. Some of the initiatives can be around the following:

1. Family day celebrations where all the family members can meet the company's employees.
2. Regular letters/emails to family members from the Leadership sharing the performance of the company and expressing their gratitude for the contribution of their family members.
3. Organizing common family get-aways for all team members.
4. Site/factory/office visits for family members.
5. Scholarship programs for children.
6. Creating an online social forum connecting the family members of all sales employees.

Truly meaningful engagement

Truly meaningful and lasting engagement is always made by the immediate manager. While it is an adage that people leave because of their managers, reverse is also true. People stay because of the way their managers engage with them. For a Sales HRBP, it is very important to continuously invest in building managerial talent in the organization by various coaching and training interventions.

Managers can engage with their team members through the following ways:

1. Creating a rhythm of individual informal connects with team members to discuss issues beyond work.
2. Creating an opportunity to have regular joint informal team connect where the team can bond with each other and the manager.
3. Be aware of the life stage the team member is in and support him/her in case he/she is in a difficult situation, sometimes by asking the organization (e.g. shortage of funds, transfers, etc.) or by individual counselling.
4. Be available for a quick discussion over a call every day to get the pulse on the ground.
5. Being honest and giving the right developmental feedback without hiding facts. This may sometimes lead to difficult conversations, but honesty will help build trust over the long term.

Measuring Engagement

Like many other softer parts, measuring the effectiveness of any engagement initiative is always very challenging for Sales HRBPs and requires extensive work. However, if one gets it right, it can lead to many advantages and ensure smooth operations.

Some of the ways to measure engagement are:

Surveys to get hard data

Sales HRBPs can launch bi-yearly or yearly engagement surveys to all the sale employees to gauge the engagement index. Many off-the-shelf tools are readily available for these surveys. Right administration of these surveys should be done to encourage honest feedback by ensuring anonymous submissions. Subjective comments should be allowed to be shared to gauge the actual emotions going on in the minds of the employees. The action areas that emerge out of the surveys should be made public and task-forces should be instituted to drive improvements.

Real time surveys

Many organizations are now adopting Artificial Intelligence Chatbox-based real time surveys to gauge ongoing employee emotions. The employees can share their feelings and emotions online (or through an app) using the chat-box as and when they want. This helps gauge the ongoing engagement index and can give insights into how this aspect is changing over a period of time, especially before and after launch of engagement initiatives.

On- ground connect

The best way to gauge engagement is to periodically visit the ground/market with sales employees and shadow with them for a few days to gauge their commitment and engagement. This along with hard surveys can form a powerful tool to understand the current levels of engagement and then further design or update any engagement initiative by working on the gaps. Sales HRBPs should make it a point to visit all supervisors once a quarter (or six months, depending on team size). He should also ensure connect over daily phone calls to understand the situation on the ground and get feedback on any of the ongoing issues. This also helps to build the rapport of the Sales HRBP and provides the employees a sounding board and an authority to trust.

Feedback from customers

An indirect feedback of customers is also a good measure to understand the engagement of the sales employees in their jobs. It takes a lot of time to build rapport with customers and if they speak positively, it is a sure win for an engaged sales employee.

An engaged and a happy employee is an asset for the organization.

Case Study:

Ana is working as a Sales HRBP in a retail company. Recently the Engagement Survey was conducted, and her unit scored the lowest. The team had strong subjective comments on manager behavior, complex company processes & low levels of salary.

a) How can Ana analyze the cause of demotivation in detail?

b) What measures can she take to create an Engagement Strategy for the team?

c) What can be the best implementable solutions for the problem areas?

Summary:

1. Having a well-defined engagement strategy for the sales team not only improves the commitment of the team, but also leads to higher talent retention.
2. Best employee engagement initiatives are those which are planned, designed, participated, performed and measured by the sales team themselves.
3. It is important to phase all these engagement activities round through the year so that the team is engaged throughout.
4. Truly meaningful and lasting engagement is always made by the immediate manager.
5. On the job working/shadowing can build the rapport of the Sales HRBP and provides the employees a sounding board and an authority to trust.

Chapter 8: Compensation & Incentives

> *"When an actor comes to me and wants to discuss his character, I say, 'It's in the script.' If he says, 'But what's my motivation?' I say, 'Your salary.'"* — *Alfred Hitchcock*

A right compensation strategy is needed for sales team to attract, motivate and retain the right talent. Compensation is a huge area and covering all aspects of compensation is beyond the scope of this book. Compensation strategy should be made on principles of transparency, fairness and compliance to local laws. Key inputs for designing the compensation strategy for the sales team are as follows:

1. Business and HR strategy.
2. Ability of the company to pay basis product portfolio, pricing and volume, etc.
3. External benchmarking with relevant companies.
4. Internal benchmarking with other functions (also known as job evaluation).
5. Prevailing government norms.

It must be mentioned that all aspects of compensation strategy need to be handled with utmost confidentiality and privacy. This is the most sensitive HR process. This also has many local laws governing the design, payout, query or grievance resolution and hence adherence to them is very important.

Compensation strategy for salesmen

Salesmen form an important part in driving the overall business strategy. Their compensation can be decided basis the below points:

1. In many countries, there are well defined norms of minimum wages which gets revised regularly based on ongoing inflation and cost of living expenses. This should be considered as the base level for ascertaining the salary range for salesmen.
2. The salary range for the salesmen should be decided based on the existing market norms and the ability of the company to pay.
3. Depending on product complexity, different categories of customers, effort needed to make the sale, number of customers to be covered, etc. the fixed part of the salary should be decided.
4. Compensation of salesmen should be competitive in the market in order to retain the salesmen. It is better to pay a little premium than to spend time and resources in hiring and onboarding new salesmen as a result of frequent attrition due to salary issues.
5. Incentives should encourage the salesmen to put more efforts to drive business and should include parameters like:
    a. Sales revenue.
    b. Market execution parameters.
    c. Billing parameters.
    d. Other business relevant KPIs.
6. The incentive criteria can have slabs, i.e. different payments for different achievement percentages.
7. In many cases, incentives are often a fixed or a

variable cut of the total sales made (e.g.- 1% of total sales done). While this can be very simple method, ensuring that the salesmen are able to sell low value range can be a bit of a challenge. In order to get numbers, a smart salesman will end up selling products having high price only.

8. Incentives should not include basic hygiene factors essential to the job like attendance, duration of work, etc. as the philosophy of incentive is to drive business performance.

9. The costs of incentive should be borne by the value generated. Softer aspects like attendance, duration of work etc. are basic to the job.

10. It is important to communicate the incentive structure to the team regularly to ensure they remained focus on the key priorities as well as can strive to earn more.

11. Compensation should also differentiate between experienced and new salesmen.

12. Over a period of time, increments in the fixed salary should be made based on performance and changes of defined minimum wages.

13. It is also important to communicate the date of salary payment and the payment of incentives (monthly/quarterly, etc.) to provide full transparency to the salesmen.

14. Any issues with respect to the salary of the salesmen need to be addressed pro-actively and with speed as most of the them come from humble background and are generally dependent on their salaries to run their household.

Compensation strategy for supervisors & managers

1. Compensation for supervisors & managers depend on the experience required for the role, complexity of territories, customer profiles, team size and the local prevailing laws.
2. It is important to conduct an external benchmarking exercise with relevant companies to understand the payment ranges and then finalize in which percentile/quartile the company can afford to pay.
3. It is also important to conduct an internal job evaluation to ascertain the hierarchy of the role within the organization. Same roles in different territories or serving different customer profiles can have different evaluation scores and hence needs to be paid differently.
4. Incentives can be around 10-25% of fixed salary and can be modified as per external benchmarking and affordability of the company.
5. The criteria for incentives need to broader at the territory level and should be focused on key drivers of business.
6. Incentive criteria should be such that it can be measured easily and authentically to determine the payments.
7. Incentive can also have slabs- different payments for different level of achievements.
8. The date of payment of the salary and frequency of incentives payment should be clearly communicated to the team.

Key points to consider during change of compensation plan or incentives

The compensation or incentive plan for the sales team can undergo a change due to changes in external or internal environment or due to promotion of the employee or change in role. There could be a new compensation strategy, or the existing strategy might have been updated. In all these situations, it is important to communicate the impact on the compensation and/or incentives to all the sales employees clearly.

Any change in compensation can evoke multiple emotional response from sales employees and hence all these communications should be handled very delicately and with empathy. A sales employee is generally keen to know what the net cash in hand will be after deducting taxes, any provident fund, etc. and hence, it is essential to make the communication in relation to this component of the salary.

Incentives also get updated on a periodic basis in many companies depending on the business strategy. Sometimes, the frequency of payout of the incentives can also get changed (e.g. change from monthly to quarterly, etc.). It is important to communicate this change a few weeks prior to the effective date so that the employee can accordingly plan to manage his/her expenses, etc.

Other compensation & benefits related inputs:

1. Matters related to compensation issues of any individual employee needs to be dealt with in a confidential manner.
2. If there are any errors in calculation of the salary or incentives, the same should be corrected as soon as possible and the correct salary must be provided to the employee.
3. It is always important to build transparency in matters related to compensation and hence any salary offer, revised salary, incentive or bonus calculations should be communicated both verbally and through a written letter. The letter should display the various components of the salary clearly.
4. Salary slips/incentive communications, etc. should be provided as per prevalent labor laws and practice in the industry.
5. Incentives data can also provide key insights into the performance of the sales employee over a period of time and hence it should be confidentially dealt.
6. Taxes arising out of incentives should be considered as per law.

Case Study:

A consumer products company has more than 2000 salesmen in a country. With the advent of bike taxis, food delivery app, etc. in the city, this company is seeing an attrition of 60% of its salesmen which is negatively impacting the business. Natalie has recently joined as the Sales HRBP for this company.

a) What measures can Natalie take to identify the reasons of the attrition?

b) How can Natalie address the compensation issues at the salesmen level?

c) Can the compensation correction of salesmen have an adverse impact on other roles?

Summary:

1. Compensation strategy should be made on principles of transparency, fairness and existing labor laws.

2. The minimum wages defined as per law should be considered as the base level for ascertaining the salary range for salesmen.

3. Incentives should not include basic hygiene factors to the job like attendance, duration of work, etc. as the philosophy of incentive is to drive business performance and not discipline.

4. For supervisors and managers compensation, it is important to conduct an external benchmarking exercise with relevant companies to understand the payment ranges and then finalize in which percentile/quartile can the company can afford to pay.

5. Any change in compensation can evoke multiple emotional responses from sales employees and hence all these communications should be handled very delicately and with empathy.

6. Matters related to compensation issues of any individual employee needs to be dealt with in a confidential manner.

Chapter 9: Attrition or Turnover Management

> *"Turnover can be one of the most expensive problems at a company"*
> *- Shawn Achor*

Attrition or turnover of sales employees impact the business directly and hence is a key hotspot for many companies. While many companies consider the costs of attrition as part of their losses in an operational business, for Sales HRBP, it can give an insight into the existing culture, manager quality, process efficiencies and effectiveness of policies.

High attrition of sales employees must be dealt with extreme caution as it may lead to considerable impact on revenues and can also waste critical time of the company in rehiring exercise. Frequent attrition also proves costly for the company. High attrition is also detrimental to company's culture and impacts the motivation of existing employees. This situation results into wastage of energies of the employees who end up spending their time in gossips and discussion on rumors. This results into a somber work environment & creates insecurity in the minds of sales employees who as such operate from a distance to the headquarters.

Common reasons for attrition of sales employees

1. **Manager quality-** Behavior of manager towards his team members is one of the key reasons why employees stay or leave the organization. In many organizations, employees do not have any way to express their feelings towards a difficult manager and this leads to their exit. In these cases, many managers escape easily by highlighting that the employee couldn't adopt well to the organization or couldn't come to speed with his performance rather than working on his manager quality.

2. **Work environment related issues-** All employees look for a healthy working environment which provides safety, flexibility, respect and recognition to the efforts of the employees. Many employees leave obnoxious working environments because they get stressed in such environments. By being a sounding board and pro-actively establishing connect with employees, Sales HRBPs can identify the improvement areas in the culture and then can work with the management to improve the same.

3. **Family related/locational issues of employees-** Sales employees, especially supervisors and salesmen do not adapt well to changes in the locations, partially because their salaries may not be sufficient to sustain livelihood in places far-away to their hometowns. The issue is further aggravated if they have any sick family member who needs care. Dual careers (of both husband and wife) can also lead to attrition. The only solution from an

employee point of view is to find another job at a location that will help solve these issues, either inside or outside the current organization.

4. **Complex business processes-** There can be a situation when the business processes are complex and leads to the sales employees spending their time on repeated non-value adding activities or puts them in a difficult situation in front of the customers. If there is no one in the organization to work on simplifying these issues, or at least give a patient hearing to the suggestions of sales employees on how to resolve them, the employee may feel frustrated and leave the company.

5. **Salary related issues-** Extended long hours of work, low pay, high amount of travel, etc. can create stress in the minds of the employees and encourage them to find easier jobs outside.

6. **Wrong hire-** If the hiring process is not able to screen the candidates properly or hiring is conducted under a hurry, a person can be hired for the wrong job resulting into attrition.

7. **Low chances of career growth-** If the organization does not have a sound career and capability building strategy, an employee can feel stuck in his/her job with no view of the future growth. In such cases, as soon as the employee finds the next challenging role outside, he leaves the organization.

8. **Safety issues-** Sales employees as such need to spend a lot of time travelling. If the territories of the employees are large in area and requires extensive travelling or if the territory itself has safety concerns, the employee might leave the company.

9. Highly ambitious **employees-** There can be a few employees who are highly ambitious, and they want to grow faster than the growth their current company can provide. It is important to identify such employees and pro-actively engage with them by giving them a transparent view of the career strategy.

10. **Other reasons specific to an industry or a particular company-** A few industries as such can have a higher rate of attrition due to the type of business they are in (e.g. software companies, consumer goods companies, etc.). Also, the higher is the transferrable skills of employees across multiple organizations, the higher will be the chances of attrition. Other reasons could be specific to a particular company owing to its culture or the mode of operation.

Categorization of talent

In order to mitigate attrition, it is important to first build a visibility on the 'talent landscape' of the existing employees. There are already several theories available on identification and categorization of talent, e.g. the 9-box model, etc. A few ways in which talent landscape can be built are as follows:

1. One can purchase an off-the-shelf solution to conduct the online or offline surveys and quickly categorize the talent. One can also ask consultants to do this work based on the local needs.
2. One can also roll-out a basic survey to all the managers to run the 'talent assessment' process by categorizing their team members in the talent boxes.
3. One will need to share the parameters (e.g. performance ratings over the past few years, manager's inputs on the potential to grow, tenure in role, tenure in organization, etc.) with the managers along with the formats to conduct the assessment.

The results of these assessments are confidential and should not be shared with individual employees.

Uses of Talent Landscape

The results of the 'talent landscape' can be used in various ways:

1. It helps to identify the spread of talent across multiple territories and across different teams
2. It can help in identifying top and poor performers. Talent and capability building measures can then be applied with different intensity and focus to sharp-shoot talent development.
3. It can help build a talent pipeline for high-performers by making the individual talent visible.
4. Those identified as concerns can be given special focus for capability building. They can also be given an opportunity to improve by involving in

various live projects, training and coaching sessions. Back-up hiring, or talent bench can be created in case they fail to perform in future.

5. A study on correlation of sales performance and talent landscape can be run to see the dependence of the same. In case the correlation coefficient is high, employees who are placed high in 'talent landscape' can be considered as bench for next level roles or promotions. They are also the ones who should be retained at all costs.

Attrition or Turnover Risk Profiling

It is important for the Sales HRPB to conduct an exercise called the "Attrition or Turnover Risk Profiling" for the entire sales team. This requires strong connect with sales employees. This exercise can have far reaching consequences in identifying the main reasons of attrition in the organization and then addressing those reasons to reduce attrition. This combined with the 'talent landscape' can provide formulation of an excellent **Talent Retention Strategy**.

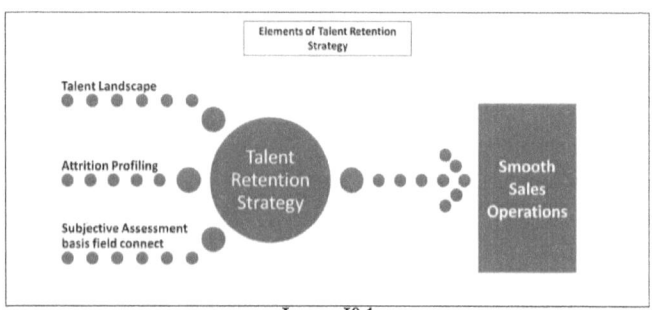

Image I9.1

How to conduct Attrition Risk Profiling?

In order to conduct Attrition Risk Profiling for the sales employees, the following methods can be used:

1. Conduct interviews of all the ex-employees who had resigned in the last 1-2 years. This interview can also be conducted by a third-party so that the former employee can share the exact reason on why he had left the company. Before conducting such interviews, it is necessary to analyze the existing data already available with the company in relation to the performance of the employee as well as his inputs given during the exit interviews.
2. It is important to analyze the subjective data as well as any objective data coming out of the above interviews to find common trends. The commonly observed trends or parameters can be categorized as:

   a. Job level/salary band/incentive issue.

   b. Manager quality.

   c. Low performing territory/Hyper-competition/Territories with social-unrest, etc.

   d. Behavior of any common colleague/co-worker/customer/partner/distributor, etc.

   e. The name of organization which they joined after resignation (maybe many of them moved together to the same organization).

   f. Any common reason (like change of salary or a particular phase in which the company was, or an organization process related issue).

   g. Hiring related issues (e.g. hiring for some territory but posting in some other territory, language issues, false communication of salary, etc.).

   h. Family related issues (distance from hometown, sickness of family members).

   i. Any other individual issues (ambition to grow faster, not willing to take multiple responsibilities, etc.).

3. Based on these inputs, one must devise a questionnaire and first ask some of the experienced managers to answer against each of the parameters. E.g., what is their take on hiring of sales employees in a particular region in which competition activities are very high, etc.

4. Get insights on the gap that exists in reality vs. the perception of experienced employees.

5. Try to create a simple ranking strategy of all these parameters, highlighting what are the top 3 reasons which had led to major attrition in the past and hence in future, may again lead to more attrition.

6. After developing and structuring this information into a tabular format, one can allocate a subjective rating (1 being low, 5 being high) to rate every

employee on each of these parameters. E.g. if the employee is having a sick family member in his hometown, one can allocate a ranking of 5, given that the employee might want to relocate to hometown to take care of the family member and hence might already be searching for a job outside in case there are no opportunities in his existing company.

7. Ratings will involve interviewing employees and connecting with employees during market visits to capture the status in each of these parameters.

8. Summation of the ratings on each of the criteria and then arranging the same in descending order for each of the employee can give an insight into the risk level of attrition for each employee.

9. Every employee can be categorized as having:

   a. **High attrition risk- Red Profile-** The employee might leave within the next 3 months.

   b. **Medium attrition risk- Amber Profile-** The employee might leave in the medium term, say around 6 months.

   c. **Low attrition risk- Green Profile-** The employee is stable in his job and is not at risk of attrition immediately.

10. Specific action plans will need to be designed for each of the above profiles.

Red Profile- Ringfencing possible attrition

1. The major parameters which are having higher ratings leading to the red profile needs to be thoroughly reviewed- is it one or two parameters leading to a red score or a mix of all?
2. For any parameter rating high, a specific action can be taken within the company norms and the employee can be communicated that the organization is looking at his concerns for resolution. But if there are many parameters leading to a red score, resolving all of them at the same time might be difficult and that sales employee will continue to be at attrition risk.
3. In such cases, a bench employee or pro-active silent hiring should be done for such roles such that in case the existing employee leaves, the new employee can join at the earliest without much gap.
4. In any cases, the existing employee should also be tried to be retained as long as possible (unless it is a consistent performance issue).

Note-

It has been observed that many sales supervisors and managers request for transfer to other locations basis their life stage issues/preference to be in proximity to home location/marriage commitments/transfer of spouse etc. Not all these requests can be immediately addressed, but the fact remains that if the movement is important, the employee will keep on searching for a job in that location and is at a high risk of attrition.

It is advisable that wherever possible, such requests should be agreed (within the organization norms and career strategy) to retain the employee. Such employees are always grateful to the company and their longevity with the company increases many folds due to measures like these. The benefit to the company is higher than the losses due to attrition.

Amber Profile-

1. The reasons for the amber profile should be analyzed in detail to understand if it is individual centric (e.g. plans for marriage) or a generic issue (e.g. a process in the company that is inefficient leading to frustration).
2. If the reasons are generic, it may lead to more amber cases in future and hence needs to be resolved in partnership with relevant functions.
3. If the issue is person specific, proper counselling should be done or possible solutions should be unlocked over a period of time.
4. It is advisable to build a bench for such cases by silent hiring or internal career strategy.

Green Profile-

1. Employees in green profile are the ones who may be engaged, motivated and be ready to take bigger assignments and projects.
2. This green status is not everlasting. Due to changes in situation (employee-related or company-related) the profile can change and hence it is important to update the rankings after every connect.

Case Study:

Louis is a Sales HRBP in a renowned pharmaceutical company. He has been seeing very high attrition of his medical representatives over the past year. This attrition is putting an additional burden on him to hire their replacements faster and on-board them quickly.

a) What can Louis do to understand the reasons of high attrition?
b) How can Louis address these issues pro-actively?
c) How can Louis help create longevity of the sales representatives in the company?

Summary:

1. High attrition of sales employees may lead to considerable impact on revenues and can also waste critical time of the company in rehiring. Hence sufficient measures should be taken to avoid this situation.

2. In order to decide on actions to reduce attrition, it is important to first understand the 'talent landscape' of the existing sales population.

3. Attrition Risk Profiling can help identify the main reasons of attrition in the organization and then those reasons can be addressed to reduce attrition.

4. Every employee can be categorized into:
    a. High attrition risk- Red Profile- The employee might leave within the next 3 months
    b. Medium attrition risk- Amber Profile- The employee might leave in the medium term, say around 6 months
    c. Low attrition risk- Green Profile- The employee is stable in his job and is not at risk of attrition immediately.

Blank Page

Chapter 10: Grievance Management & Ethics

> *"You can't hold on to a grievance and be happy. Time to make a choice!"*
> *- Robert Holden*

Employee grievances are part and parcel of an operating business. However, it is generally left to the immediate manager to resolve them in the manner they think is fit. Grievance handling is one of the key aspects of having a large sales team and can have a major impact the engagement levels of the employees. It is important to provide a structured 'grievance resolution mechanism' so that all grievances can first be heard and then satisfactorily resolved.

For Sales HRBPs, grievances can also give an insight into what could be the improvement areas for the organization. Any area from where the grievances come time and again can become the precursor to a bigger issue and therefore, it is important to have a well-defined 'grievance resolution mechanism' in the organization.

In many countries there are established laws around handling grievances of the employees. Where there aren't any, one can always look to implement the 'grievance resolution mechanism' in a simple manner to resolve any employee issues and keep the team engaged and happy.

Key aspects of 'Grievance Resolution Mechanism'

1. For the sales team, an online or a call based 'grievance resolution mechanism' can be established using an off-the shelf solution or developing it easily using online customizable forms (e.g. Google forms, etc.).
2. The entire process of grievance resolution should be laid out in a logical and time-bound manner. The same should be communicated to employees regularly.
3. All grievances should be tracked, updated in a periodic meeting by a grievance committee comprising of cross-functional team members.
4. There has to be a defined turn-around-time for all grievance resolution and the status of the same should be made visible to the person who is raising the grievance.
5. It is best to give an option to the employee to either declare his/her name while raising a grievance or keep it anonymous. In case there is an issue related specific to an individual (e.g. wrong calculation of incentives, etc.), the employee can furnish his/her name so that the specific issue can be pin-pointed and resolved.
6. An analysis of type of grievances should be done periodically to understand if there are common themes or trends coming out of it. If there is, that issue must be addressed logically to avoid any possible grievances in future.
7. All grievances and their solutions should be recorded and must not be deleted. In many situations, they also serve a legal record.

8. Quick closure of employee grievances increases the trust of the employee in the organization and makes them believe that there is someone to listen to them and take care of them.

Type of Grievances of sales employees

The nature and types of grievances of sales employees can vary depending on the type of the company, internal issues, organization and country culture, etc. Some of them can revolve around:

1. Compensation related issues-

An employee might want to know about the various components of his salary, how is it calculated, any absenteeism days, salary payment dates, reason for delay in payment of salaries, salary not received, insurance coverage, etc. Employees can also raise query on the quantum of their salaries to ask for a raise or a promotion.

2. Incentives issues-

Employees can raise grievances over their incentive payout, calculation of incentive, any delay in payouts etc. As incentive is part of compensation structure and paid in cash in many companies, sales employees generally account to receive the same as part of their salary structure and accordingly plan their expenses. If there is an issue over this, it might not only cause a grievance but also impact their motivation to perform.

3. Bad behavior of colleague/manager-

This is one of the most common but serious type of grievance. In many cultures, employees generally hesitate to give any negative feedback to their manager or colleagues upfront and keep the feelings to themselves. This keeps on going till the time the person feels that he cannot continue anymore in the organization. Such grievances are an important indicator of the manager quality and the existing sales culture beyond the walls of the office and must be addressed in a mature way by identifying the root cause of the grievance and then counselling the relevant manager/colleague or the reportee (as the case may be).

4. Any personal issues-

Requests for transfers, change in role, promotion, etc. can arise out of personal ambition or need. It must be addressed as per the norms.

5. Any process related issues-

Employees can give feedback on the various processes (distributor claims processing, product quality, delayed responsiveness by some department/person, etc.) which needs to be addressed as required.

Ethics in Sales

Sales employees represent their organization and at many times are the only person from the organization interacting with customers/clients. The way they deal with the customers represents the culture, practices and the norms in which the organization operates and hence, it important to be transparent in dealings and uphold ethics of business with the customers. Sales HRBPs should ensure that there are regular trainings on the values, code of conduct and norms of operating the business and guidelines on do's and don'ts of behavior for the sales employees. These guidelines are not limited to only dealing with customers but should be equally valid when dealing with anyone within the company or outside it (vendors, partners, etc.).

Anonymous helpline for whistleblowers

It is of utmost importance to establish an anonymous call based and/or an online helpline for raising issues that violate the ethical norms of the company. This increases trust of all the stakeholders in the company as well as provides a critical way to raise issues that can harm the business. Issues raised through this helpline need to be addressed quickly by an independent committee and records must be preserved.

Case Study:

Vikram is one of the existing customers who has been dealing with the sales representative- John for two years. Vikram had ordered a certain quantity of the product that John sells which were delivered on time but were short in quantity. John is unwilling to accept that the product was supplied in short quantity citing that he had counted the same himself before dispatch.

a) What can Vikram do in this situation?
b) What can John do in this situation?
c) How can this organization resolve such issues?

Summary:

1. Grievance redressal is generally left to the immediate manager for resolution, which may not be adequate. Sales HRBPs should provide the right framework to address grievances.
2. Any area from where the grievances are coming time and again can become the precursor to a bigger issue.
3. There has to be a defined turn-around-time for all grievance resolution.
4. All grievances and their solutions should be recorded and must not be deleted/destroyed.
5. The way the sales employees deal with the customers represents the culture, practices and the norms in which the organization operates and hence it important to be transparent in dealings and uphold Ethics of business with the customers.
6. It is of utmost importance to establish an anonymous call based and/or an online helpline for raising issues that defy the Ethical norms for employees, customers and partners

Chapter 11: Safety & Legal Considerations

> *"For safety is not a gadget but a state of mind."*
> *— Eleanor Everest*

Safety of employees is of paramount importance and no organization can succeed if it can't provide a safe working environment to its employees. The matter of safety is not limited to offices or factories or retail stores and there are many laws in many countries, where the transit from home to office and vice versa and even the route to market is considered as an extension of workplace. If any incident happens while working in the market or visiting a customer, it may be liable to get covered in the medical insurance provided by the organization as well as be reported in the Annual Report disclosure.

As sales employees spend a lot of time travelling, ensuring their safety while travelling is always a company's prerogative. Any company will need to have defined processes to on-board any new sales employees on safety norms as well as periodically train their existing sales team members. The following safety related topics can be used for training:

1. Road safety norms.
2. Right way of driving any vehicle (motorbike, car,

truck, etc.).

3. Do's and Don'ts while being on road (e.g. avoid talking on mobile phone while driving).
4. Importance of wearing seat belts in four wheelers/helmets for two wheelers.
5. Importance of keeping the vehicle well maintained
6. Safe driving norms- speed limits, maintaining distance between two vehicles, etc.
7. Response assistance during any emergency situation like-
   a. Road accidents.
   b. Vehicle on fire.
   c. Road rage of fellow drivers.
   d. Any police related issues.
8. Emergency helplines numbers for any safety related matters should be shared with the all sales team members.
9. Details of their insurance/medical coverage should be made available to them.
10. Names and addresses of recommended hospitals with whom the organization has tie-up should be shared with the employees.

Providing medical coverage/Insurance

It is a healthy practice to provide medical insurance to all the sales employees, including salesmen. While in many countries, the same is already mandated as per employment laws, in other countries even if it is not mandated, the company should decide to provide medical support/insurance to all the sales employees.

There are several benefits to it:

1. It increases the trust of the employees in the company.
2. In case of any dire situation, the employees are covered financially.
3. Any financial impact because of accidents, etc. will not impact the company as the same will be covered by the insurance.
4. Employees can also avail paid leaves from the coverage to recuperate and in many insurance norms.
5. The company also protects itself legally from litigation, etc. by availing insurance coverage for the employees.

Other employment laws for sales employees

Many countries have specific laws/Acts defining the employment, service conditions, termination, etc. for sales employees. It is important that the Sales HRBPs implement these rules and regulations of the land for sales employees. It is generally seen that the adherence of laws is higher for factory locations or retain stores, etc. owing to constant scrutiny of government officials as compared to sales employees as they are geographically spread. But this can't be an excuse to not implement the rules of the land. It is the onus of Sales HRBPs to not only mitigate any legal issues arising out of such matters, but also generate a trust in the employees and the environment that the company is a law adhering entity. Some of the ways in which this can be implemented are:

1. Create a list of Acts/Rules applicable to different roles of the sales employees.
2. Do periodic (say monthly) audits of these Acts/rules with the team and share the result with the Management. Ensure you include sales managers as partners in this activity to drive accountability and ownership.
3. The different rules can be categorized as low risk, medium risk or high risk, depending on the impact to the business as well as the penalties involved.
4. Over a period, all rules should be adhered to. Sufficient awareness will also need to be made by regular training sessions on legal aspects for employees and partners.
5. One can also look at hiring external consultants who can do periodic audits for the company and share mitigation plans to improve compliance.

Prevention of Sexual Harassment

As sales employees are spread across the geography, it is very important to implement the rules of Prevention of Sexual Harassment as per the existing laws. It is important to make all the employees aware of these rules as well as provide a redressal mechanism to resolve any escalations. It is also advisable to institute a Committee for investigation & redressal of complaints of this nature constituting of women and men, internal and a few external members certified to handle such issues. As Sales HRBPs, it is advisable to escalate any issues pertaining to such matter to the Committee for investigation. The committee should be given a free-hand to decide on the matter and subsequently advise appropriate actions.

Case Study:

One of the salesmen- George suffered a road accident while he was on the way to meet his customer. He had a fracture on his leg and required a surgery at the local hospital. He was not covered under any insurance scheme or medical coverage provided by the company.

His manager- Jeff has also refused to provide any support to George citing that George was on 3rd party rolls and not on the Company rolls because of which he was not eligible for medical insurance coverage by the company.

1. What can George or his family members do in this situation?
2. Is there any risk to the Company?
3. What impact can it have on other salesmen?

Summary:

1. The matter of safety is not limited to offices or factories, it extends to all sales employees working in the markets, both as a moral responsibility as well as mandated in a few countries as per law.

2. It is always a company's prerogative to ensure safety of sales employees. Periodic training and awareness of various safety aspects are important.

3. The company should provide the Emergency helplines numbers for any safety related matters along with the insurance details of every employee.

4. It is important that the Sales HRBPs implement the rules and regulations of employment and maintain proper service conditions of sales employees as per existing law and by having a structured process.

.

Chapter 12: Retirement/Termination

> *"The services of any employee may be terminated but based on a "established reasonable ground" and not just any nebulous raison d'être."*
> — *Henrietta Newton Martin*

Hiring and firing of the employee is perhaps the two most precarious HR processes that can lead to litigation issues and hence both needs to be handled with utmost carefulness and caution. There are always local labor laws that dictate the termination process for any employee, and it must always be followed without any exception.

Many times, there is a pressure from the business to let go of a non-performing employee or anyone who has committed a serious misconduct and hire another person quickly to ensure business continuity. However, speeding up things and executing a termination without due diligence may unnecessarily leave a bad taste in the mind of the employee, bring dis-repute to the company as well as open the doors for lengthy litigation proceedings.

Although it is one of the tough situations for a Sales HRBP or for any other professional, termination is part and parcel of running the HR operations as per the established rules and laws of the country. A few things that can be done by the Sales HRBPs to handle such situations professionally are-

1. The reason for terminating any employee must be well established and suitable time and opportunity must be given to the employee to explain his side of the story as part of the principles of natural justice.
2. There should always be an internal independent committee who should have the final say on termination related matters and the case should be presented to this committee for final decision.
3. Termination should never be a single person's decision and enough evidences should be considered before deciding any tough action like this. In absence of hard proof, termination should not be executed, and the onus is on Sales HRBPs to push back as well as present the risks to the company if the management still insists.
4. These evidences should also be preserved for future reference. All local labor laws must be adhered to before execution of the termination.
5. During the termination discussion, it is important to present the facts of the case to the employee and the reasoning which has led to the decision in a transparent manner.
6. Sometimes, depending on the situation, it is also a good practice to present the facts of the case and give an option to the employee to resign voluntarily. A voluntary resignation in many countries is more respectful as compared to termination by the company. In many countries, as per law, the employee might also lose his right to a few components of his salary if he gets terminated.

7. Enough time should be given to the employee for discussion and it should not be a hurried thing. The self-respect of the employee should always be preserved during such tough discussions. It should not be portrayed as a personal decision by the Sales HRBPs as this can promote enmity and put the HRBPs safety at risk.

8. There can be cases in which the employee displays his anger or becomes violent. Such cases must be pro-actively planned for and enough measures should be taken to preserve the safety of oneself, other employees and the assets of the company.

9. In case of economic circumstances requiring the company to undertake lay-offs or downsizing, it is a good practice to hire an outplacement agency to support the employees in finding another opportunity as well as providing counselling. Sales HRBPs can also look at personally recommending a few employees to other known HR team members of other companies.

Retirement

Retirement as we know is act of leaving one's job when one has reached the retirement age as per the definitions of the laws of the country or as mentioned in the employment contract. Reaching at this stage, indicates the loyalty of the employee towards the company and this process must be handled with utmost sincerity and respect.

Sales HRBPs have the onus of ensuring that all retiring employees get the opportunity to meet the management team and all other employees before the last day of the retiring employee. A memento or a farewell gift should always be arranged as per the company policy for retiring employees.

The 'full and final' payments including all statutory dues (like provident fund, etc.) should be processed on priority for retiring employees so that they are not short of funds. Sales HRBPs should ensure that this doesn't get missed.

A post retirement connect/alumni connect should be established to ensure well-being and continued relationship with retired employees. Other ways to engage with them could be to organize talks with current employees at regular intervals, inviting their families to the office, etc.

A retired employee continues to be the brand ambassador of the company and must always be dealt with respect.

Case Study:

Mike is working as a HRBP for a chain of retail stores employing more than 500 sales representatives operating out of these stores. Mike's office is in the same premise as that of their largest store along with the management team in GK Road. One fine afternoon, his Sales Director calls him and says that he is disappointed with one of the sales representatives- Jacob in the GK Road Store and wants Mike to fire him for non-performance. It seemed a bit surprising for Mike as he knows Jacob very well. Although Jacob is known for speaking his mind, his performance records are all clean. On preliminary discussion, it came out the Jacob had an altercation with the CEO a few days back.

a) What should Mike do in this situation?
b) Should Mike fire Jacob? How will this action be perceived by other employees?
c) What are the risks?
d) If Mike doesn't fire Jacob, how will his relations with the CEO get impacted?

Summary:

1. Hiring and firing of the employee is perhaps the two most precarious HR processes that can lead to litigation issues and hence, both needs to be handled with utmost carefulness and caution.

2. Speeding up things and executing a termination without due diligence may unnecessarily leave a bad taste in the mind of the employee, bring disrepute to the company as well as open the doors for long and lengthy litigation.

3. Termination should never be a single person's decision and enough evidences should be considered before deciding any tough action like this.

4. It is also a good practice to present the facts of the case, discuss with the employee and give the option to the employee to resign voluntarily.

5. Retirement indicates the loyalty of the employee towards the company and must be handled with utmost sincerity and respect.

6. The full and final payments including all statutory dues (like provident fund, etc.) should be processed on priority for retiring employees so that they are not short of funds. Sales HRBPs should ensure that this doesn't get missed.

Chapter 13: Managing Across Cultures & Countries

> *"Culture is the name for what people are interested in, their thoughts, their models,*
> *the books they read and the speeches they hear"* –
> *Walter Lippmann.*

Many multi-national companies have sales teams spread across many countries. Any Sales HRBP taking care of a multi-country role needs to understand and include the elements of the local culture in designing and implementing any Sales HR strategy. Any strategy that works with a certain set of people in one country, may not work with the other set of people in the other country due to the prevalent country and organization culture.

Key points to keep in mind while working with different cultures

1. A good place to start is to understand Hofstede's cultural dimensions theory[3] in details and then identify the current countries the HRBP is handling in the spectrum across these dimensions. This will help in understanding the existing norms

---

[3] https://www.hofstede-insights.com/product/compare-countries/

before diving deep into interactions and learning by making mistakes.

2. It will be important to have a thorough study of the existing work practices, cultural norms and ways of working. Appointing a local employee to assist the new leaders/Sales HRBP in on-boarding and answering any basic questions or connecting with other employees will help.

3. It is very important to listen more and understand the way in which the team prefers to work before initiating any change management initiatives. Spending the first 90 days to observe rather than change is advisable.

4. Another way could be to take inputs from expats working in those countries to understand the mode of operations and the existing practices of the sales team.

5. While lifting and shifting best practices from one country is the easiest way to do things, the cultural aspects can totally de-rail the same if flexibility is not provided to the team to include the local nuances. The local team should be given the opportunity to think and propose solutions to resolve any business issue, rather than just lifting and shifting from another country.

6. Learning the local language can be advantageous for the new manager as it will build the trust in the local team that efforts are being taken to understand their culture, as well as help in any future communications.

7. Any verbal or written communication in English should be followed by communication in the local language. All training materials, etc. can be translated into local language for better

understanding.

8. Local customs, hours of working, norms of leaves, holidays, etc. should be understood in detail before making any policy related decisions.

9. In many countries, the employees may not consider it polite to speak much in meetings, especially in front of senior team members. In such cases, it might be difficult to get a true feedback on initiatives in the meeting. It is important to develop an alternate way to connect to seek feedback through informal means.

10. It will also be important to understand how other relevant organizations plan their Sales HR Strategy and what can be the do's and don'ts given the local cultural norms. A benchmarking study on this can help build a robust Sales HR Strategy.

11. It is very important to understand the local labor laws before implementing any initiatives impacting people.

Case Study:

Samantha has recently moved from a one country Sales HRBP role to a multi-country Sales HRBP role. She had successfully implemented many end to end processes for hiring, capability building and engagement in her previous role and wants to establish herself quickly in the new role by having quick wins. She is planning to replicate her work in these HR processes in the new role.

a) What all aspects should Samantha consider before she implements the best practices in her new role?
b) Should she implement them as soon as possible or wait it out?
c) What can be risks if the local team don't buy-in the new processes?

Summary:

1. Any Sales HRBP taking care of multi-country role needs to understand and include the elements of the local culture in designing and implementing any Sales HR Strategy.

2. Understanding Hofstede's cultural dimensions theory could be a good way to learn about different aspects of culture.

3. While lifting and shifting best practices from one country is the easiest way to do things, the cultural aspects can totally de-rail the same if flexibility is not provided to the team to include the local nuances.

4. It is very important to understand the local labor laws before implementing any initiatives impacting people.

Chapter 14: Preparing for Uncertain Business Situations

> *"The mistake is thinking that there can be an antidote to the uncertainty."*
> *- David Levithan*

As I am writing this book in 2020, an unpredicted and unprecedented pandemic situation (COVID-19) has brought the world economy and human life to a near standstill. Existing businesses will face uncertain moments and the role of Sales HRBP will become even more important. Employees will look at the HR colleagues for support in this crisis situation.

Businesses can prepare themselves to adapt to uncertain situations like:

1. A natural calamity like a hurricane, earthquake, volcanic eruption, etc.

2. Wars between nations or within nations.

3. An epidemic/pandemic.

4. Sudden Death of the proprietor.

5. Circumstances driven change in consumer

preferences (e.g. home delivery of food vs. eating out).

6. Demonetization by the Government.

7. Any internal scam/wrong reporting of financials/frauds/lawsuits, etc.

8. Loss of assets- fire in the plant, bankruptcy, etc.

9. Sudden aggression of competition, introduction of a new technology/cheaper variant, changes in import/export laws, etc.

10. Any other crisis.

How can Sales HRBP support business and people by pro-actively planning for such situations?

1. The number one priority at all times for the Sales HRBP should be the safety and security of the sales team. As the team is spread across geography and there is limited daily interaction with each and every member of the sale team, suitable **Disaster Management Protocol** should be made to ascertain the safety of all employees.

2. These protocols should be part of the on-boarding plan as well as regular awareness sessions should be conducted to make the employee aware on the guidelines.

3. Processes should be set up so that each employee can report his well-being on a real time basis (maybe an app, 24x7 helpline number, etc.) and the same can be tracked if any crisis hits the company.

4. If any employee is stuck in a crisis situation, suitable methods should be established to provide support to the employee (tie-up with hospitals, air-lifting support, etc.).

5. A task-force should be established on who will review the developments at a set frequency and take necessary executive decisions.

6. Scenario planning should be conducted to understand how the situation can evolve. Plans should be made citing the actions that need to be taken for each scenario.

7. It is of utmost importance to maintain strong & frequent communication between the management, the task force and all the employees through various channels.

8. In situations where life is not at threat (e.g. a financial fraud, etc.), suitable measures should be taken to explain the situation to the employees and the actions that the management is planning to take to resolve the issue. In absence of the same, employees might feel insecure.

9. Clear guidelines need to be issued on who can interact with media, government officials, etc. during any crisis situation.

10. Further there should be guidelines issued on the dos and don'ts of the social media behavior to avoid spreading of any fake news by any employee.

11. A bigger doubt that persists in the minds of any employee is with respect to his or her continuity in the job with the company. Everything said and

done, a large percentage of salaried team members are economically dependent on their jobs. Any crisis, either in the company or in the environment, can send the emotions of the employees into a vicious spiral. It is very important to be transparent in such times and communicate the exact reality to the employees.

12. The Sales HRBP should be accessible 24x7 in such situations.

Case Study:

There was an earthquake in the city on a working day when the sales employees were working in the market. Alex was working as the Sales HRBP. While the earthquake was not massive, the CEO had asked Alex to take stock of the situation and report any issues.

a) What can Alex do in this situation?
b) Assuming there are no past precedents of such a situation, what can Alex do to be prepared for the future?

Summary:

1. Businesses in the past and in the future will face uncertain moments where the role of Sales HRBP will become even more important.
2. People will look at the HR colleagues for support in the crisis situations.
3. The number one priority at all times for the Sales HRBP should be the safety and security of the sales team.
4. A **Disaster Management Protocol** should be planned to ascertain the safety of all employees.
5. It is of utmost importance to maintain strong and frequent communication between the management, the task force and all the employees through various channels during the times of the crisis.
6. Clear guidelines need to be issued on who can interact with media, government officials, etc. during any crisis situation.

Epilogue

As mentioned in this book, there are multiple facets of HR that needs to be effectively managed for the sales team. The role of Sales HRBP is not any easy one. It requires speed, flexibility and an urge to get a first-hand experience by spending more time in the market with salesmen and supervisors. It is in no way a desk role.

As we move ahead of 2020, several challenges will lie in front of sales organizations, especially for the ones for whom the 'feet on street' is important. The core way of approaching the customers in many companies is not going to change much (despite the rise in work from home or digital working) as orders will still need to be taken, shelves will still need to be merchandized and delivery of products will still need to be done. A few aspects can be supplemented by digital means (e.g. tele/app-based ordering), but the core of selling will still remain dependent on people knocking the doors of existing and potential customers day in and day out.

Focus on people will increase manifold post this period and organizations who have robust people processes will stand out and will have the first right to success.

All the best!

About the Author

Ritesh Agarwal is a professional in the field of Human Resources. He has over a decade of experience in Human Resources Management and has taken several Leadership HR Roles in sales and in manufacturing in in a prominent FMCG company. He has worked in a variety of generalist and specialist HR positions of increasing complexity across South-East Asia. He has led HR teams across geographies and has exposure to international business through multiple leadership assignments across various countries in Asia.

Ritesh has been working very closely with Business Leaders, especially sales to define the Strategic HR Agenda in various markets. He has also driven focused Learning & Development Strategies for Sales to achieve consistent business results across geographies.

Ritesh is an MBA (Human Resources) from XLRI, Jamshedpur, India, B. Tech. (Electronics & Communication Engineering, VNIT, Nagpur, India) and is also a SHRM-SCP & ATD-CPLP. He was born and brought up in Kolkata, India. He is currently based out of Bangkok, Thailand and can be reached at inspire@riteshagarwal.org.

Blank Page

Visit

www.riteshagarwal.org

to know more about his thoughts
on managing Human Resources.